Blockchain and Deep Learning Architectures for Secure IoT Systems

Srilata

TABLE OF CONTENTS

CHAPTER 1

Introduction

1.1 Overview

The Internet of Things' development has transformed a number of industries like virtual and physical systems, intelligent grids, medical services, and agricultural. The IoT network consists of sensing devices like laser scanners, temperature detectors, and RFID tags to communicate automatically and to collect the data effectively and also monitor the real-time. The large volumes of data were produced by connected devices due to huge development of IoT technologies that makes reliable structures for safe communication and data transfer (Almutairi et al., 2024). The significant barrier to preserve data integrity and user confidentiality is the intrinsic risks of IoT networks.

The reliable data transfer and addressed the data scalability issue and also reduced the latency is key obstacles in IoT-based system. The IoT devices remotely accessed and ongoing surveillance of patients, traditional has developed become a smart model (Abdulmalek et al. 2022). The IoT networks were vulnerable to attacks such as infiltration assaults that jeopardize private medical data, because of their unreliable communication method. The usefulness of existing IDS has been limited high FAR and unsatisfactory detection rate, despite their efforts to reduce these risks (Akkaş et al. 2020, Pulimamidi et al. 2022). Blockchain technology provides decentralization, confidentiality, and accessibility to data transfers as a viable alternative to improve security, integrity, and adaptability. The Smart Contracts (SC) further increase confidence by facilitating safe and verified connections among IoT devices like remote fetal tracking, thermometers, blood pressure monitors, optical scanners, and glucose levels tracking (Deepak et al., 2024).

The Incorporation blockchain with DL models shows significant potential to protect the IoT-based system (Vhatkar et al. 2026). The blockchain-based anonymity models reduce security risks and improve privacy of information by using cryptographic techniques to store the decentralized record of operations (Al-Khatib et al., 2026). The confidential health records are protected using integration of an Ethereum-based Blockchain infrastructure and make the data storage safe and unchangeable. The utilization of Generative Adversarial Networks (GANs), BiLSTM, and attention technique improves attack detection and classification accuracy (Vhatkar et al. 2026, Almalki et al. 2024, Kumar et al. 2021).

The sustainable conversation protocols like MQTT are widely used due to the need for efficient data exchange and interconnection in IoT networks and coincided with advancements in IoT-based system. The client-server architecture of conventional IoT platforms restricts scalability and raises network costs. By switching to a peer-to-peer P/S model. The constraints can be addressed and IoT devices can now generate and utilize data, increasing compatibility and effectiveness. It enables dependable and low-latency message transmission, MQTT obtained popularity in a number of sectors such as energy management and industrial automation. There are a number of specific technical issues that combined the MQTT with current LoRaWAN protocols, such as Duty-Cycle–Induced Scalability Limitation, Broker-Centric Congestion and Queueing Delay, and Propagation and Publish Delay Accumulation. The issues to maximize scalability and reduce propagation delays (Singh et al., 2026).

This work shows the comprehensive solution to secure the IoT-based system and also secure data transmission across diverse IoT applications. The proposed model not only enhances security and privacy but also addresses scalability and energy efficiency concerns that shows the way for the next generation of resilient IoT ecosystems.

1.2 Background of IoT

In overall world the millions of IoT-connected devices were continuously transfer the data to preserve the security and integrity of data. Attackers stole about USD 1.7 billion worth of digital currencies from websites in 2023 according to the Chainalysis 2024 Crypto Crime Report. The security vulnerabilities in blockchain ecosystems such as private key misuse, automated contract scams, instant loan attacks, and cross-chain connection problems are more dangerous. These incidents also demonstrate that, while the blockchain ledgers themselves are secure, implementation issues and protocol vulnerabilities constitute a significant security challenge for blockchain-based applications. How can we utilize Artificial Intelligence (AI) to strengthen digital security and keep current with intruders as the banking sector depends steadily on Bitcoin and cyberattacks become more complex?

The IDS uses network flow data to categorize the behavior in every system as either "harmful" or "legal". Unusual risks are difficult for IDS to identify, improve efficiency, and lower false alarms. These issues arise because there is a lack of assessment and verification of data. The detection of attacks based on anomalies is getting better. Bloomberg predicts that the 1.9 trillion dollars of events in 2020 will occur three times (Zalte et al. 2020). Connected electronics and organizations are more susceptible to intrusions. Scholars are offering more tenable options. As a result, identification and prevention systems need to be quick, effective, and palatable. The massive data generated from IoT devices could be resolved by data mining. An adaptable design is provided by Machine Learning (ML). These systems "learn" on their own without guidance. They could be used in a variety of security breach scenarios, particularly with IoT devices. Life is getting cheaper and increasingly opulent as actual things get faster, smarter, internet-connected, and capable of conversing without people. Web-connected devices gave rise to the idea of the IoT.

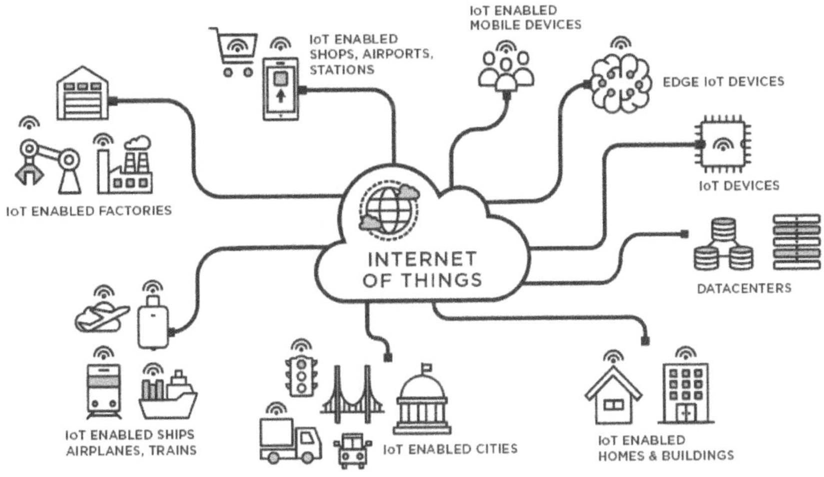

Fig. 1.1 Application of IoT

The various uses of IoT items, which comprise all everyday internet-connected equipment, are depicted in Figure 1.1. Smart devices will become indispensable because of household automation, cognitive offices, intelligent grids, and health care related to agriculture, transport, and urban areas. Although there are many benefits to IoT devices, cybersecurity remains the largest obstacle. Usability is given precedence over security, earnings, and time to market by device manufacturers. Security is ignored, and security breaches have affected people's lives on a daily basis due to their reliance on smart devices. Programs and devices increase remote connectivity and effectiveness in a variety of fields, including healthcare, transport, power plant infrastructure, irrigation plant frameworks, and electrical infrastructure.

Important facilities, including nuclear, energy, and irrigation, are using connected devices increasingly, which raises the possibility of cyber-attacks notwithstanding their computer system flaws. However, these essential services could be jeopardized if the apps are used in conjunction with Mirai, the initial widespread Distributed Denial-of-Service (DDoS) assault that used more than 32,000 connected devices. The Mirai attack used hard-coded login credentials, standard passwords, and unprotected ports to attack millions of connected devices. This attack exhibited characteristics similar to the Buzz Bot malware, an earlier IoT botnet that exploited weak authentication mechanisms and unpatched firmware to compromise large numbers of consumer IoT devices. In both cases, the attacks leveraged default credentials, insecure communication channels, and limited device-level security controls to rapidly propagate across heterogeneous IoT environments. The recent security analyzes indicate that billions of IoT devices remain vulnerable due to approximately 21 widely exploited software and firmware vulnerabilities, enabling attackers to bypass traditional perimeter defenses. Even advanced firewalls and conventional IDS are often insufficient to protect IoT infrastructures, as these systems are primarily designed for traditional IT networks and fail to account for the unique characteristics of IoT traffic. Social media sites and online business dealings have expanded. Now we urgently need network safety for these two problems. Networks continue to be dangerous in spite of all attempts to protect them. Administrators must therefore safeguard the infrastructure and ensure a rapid recovery. Tiny online groups might be capable of self-defense. Digital assaults are challenging to prevent because of the rapid advancement of phishing techniques and the variety of hacking methods available. Any system can be hacked by an attacker with enough time and capabilities; but network break-ins are the biggest concern. It is possible to use brute force, network infiltration, or outside Denial-of-Service (DoS) assaults. These jeopardizes the access, security, and security of the system. As internet traffic patterns evolve, a more flexible approach is required to identify and stop intrusions (Zalte et al. 2020).

In the IoT-based security monitoring system, each hardware and software component, such as sensors, gateways, and network nodes, is assigned a Unique Identification Number (UID) to enable precise device identification, authentication, and traceability within the network. In recent years, IoT systems have rapidly evolved due to advancements in continuous monitoring technologies, the integration of AI, and the availability of cost-effective sensing devices. Modern sensor networks deployed in residential and industrial environments are typically wireless, computationally embedded, and centrally managed, enabling large-scale data collection and real-time monitoring.

By continuously analyzing real-time network traffic data, the IDS employing an automated and intelligent system can detect whether a network is under attack by identifying deviations from normal traffic behavior patterns (Aljabri et al. 2021).

The effective detection rates are obtained using ML-based models in IDS that need high-quality training data. in the preprocessing step remove the noise, handling missing values, and levelling feature patterns. The classification accuracy and computing efficiency adversely affected by the large amount of duplicated or irrelevant information in network traffic data. The techniques used to select relevant features that reduced the dimensionality of data are necessary to preserve most informative features because not all retrieved attributes significantly aid in attack detection.

An IDS maintains surveillance on the network's data for suspicious activities and alert users. The IDS system to identify anomalies have the ability to respond to suspicious activity by blocking connections from vulnerable IP ports. The IDS to recognize unusual events and also IDS employ a range of techniques to find potentially dangerous activity. Finding anomalies and recognizing signatures are the two main uses for this method. A signature-based intrusion detection system compares the received data with known attack patterns. By examining variations in network flow behavior, anomalous traffic patterns are found using the ML-based anomaly detection technique (Muneer et al. 2024).

1.3 Machine Learning

The majority of businesses develop by using data that requires automation for anomaly detection in network. ML algorithms forecast outcomes, identify patterns, and make decisions by examining huge datasets to (Muneer et al. 2024, Aljabri et al. 2021).

1.3.1 Types of Learning

Supervised Learning: This type of learning model trained on the on labeled datasets. Each input corresponds to a known output. The model learns to generalized patterns and capture the relationships across the input-output to make predictions on unseen data. Supervised learning is widely used in classification task such as diagnosis of diseases from medical images and also used in regression analysis such as prediction of stock prices. The most popular ML models are Support Vector Machines (SVM), Decision Trees (DT), Random Forests (RF), and Deep Neural Networks (DNN) (Aljabri et al. 2021, Zhang et al. 2021).

Unsupervised Learning: This type of learning model analyze data without labeled responses to identify hidden patterns. It is commonly used to cluster the data like segmenting customers based on purchasing behavior, anomaly detection, and dimensionality reduction. The most unsupervised techniques such as K-Means, Density-Based spatial clustering of Applications with Noise, Hierarchical Clustering, and Autoencoders are frequently employed in unsupervised learning tasks (Mirsky et al. 2018, Aljabri et al. 2021).

Reinforcement Learning (RL): This learning paradigm involves an agent interacting with an environment to maximize cumulative rewards. Through trial and error, the agent learns optimal strategies or policies to achieve specific goals. RL is extensively applied in autonomous systems, robotics, game playing (AlphaGo), and financial trading. Key components of RL include the agent, environment, actions, rewards, and policies. Algorithms such as Q-Learning, Deep Q Networks (DQN), and Policy Gradient Methods are widely used for RL-based decision-making applications (Muneer et al. 2024, Aljabri et al. 2021).

1.4 Deep Learning

The ToN-IoT threats correspond to diverse cyber-attacks represented in the ToN-IoT dataset, such as DDoS, ransomware, and data exfiltration attacks targeting IoT and Industrial Internet of Things (IIoT) environments. The DL-based techniques are employed for their detection due to their ability to model complex traffic patterns and handle large-scale network data effectively.

1.4.1 Convolutional Neural Networks (CNN)

Image categorization improves with CNN. Excellent stability solutions remain to be made using the CNN approach. CNN imitates a network of neurons.

Convolutional Layered: Throughout training, the convolutional layer becomes responsible for data investigation, size, and filtration. Kernels are a kind of filtering used in this level. The effectiveness of the kernel can be improved by adjusting three crucial hyperparameters such as kernel size, number of filters, and stride/padding configuration. Minimizing neural network architecture and enhancing its efficiency can be achieved by selecting the right hyperparameter settings. Figure 1.2 shows the layers of the CNN technique Zhang et al. (2021). The dimension of the kernel was adjusted to 5, and the filtering values of 64 and 128 were utilized again. The values "a few" and "1" are assigned to the padded and durations variables.

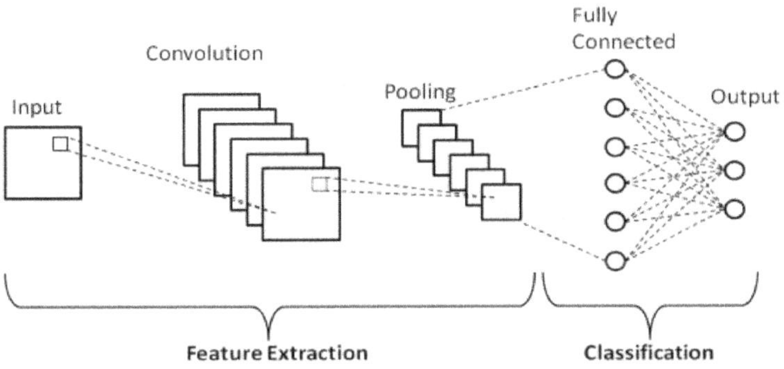

Fig 1.2 Typical Architecture of CNN (Gu et al. 2019)

$$x_i = f(w_i * x_i - 1 + b_i) \quad (1.1)$$

A convolution procedure (f) is performed during which X represents a portion used as data for input, b is the network's learning base, -1 is the outcome of the previous layer, and X represents the weighted vector. It makes utilization of a non-linear activation mechanism that is $ReLU$. This $ReLU$ operates on convolutional-layered maps of characteristics element-by-element. For negative numbers and x, $ReLU$ returns 0 as shown in Figure 1.3.

$$ReLU(x) = [0, if\ x < 0\ x, if\ z >= 0] \quad (1.2)$$

And for positive values the $ReLU$ function is 0–infinity.

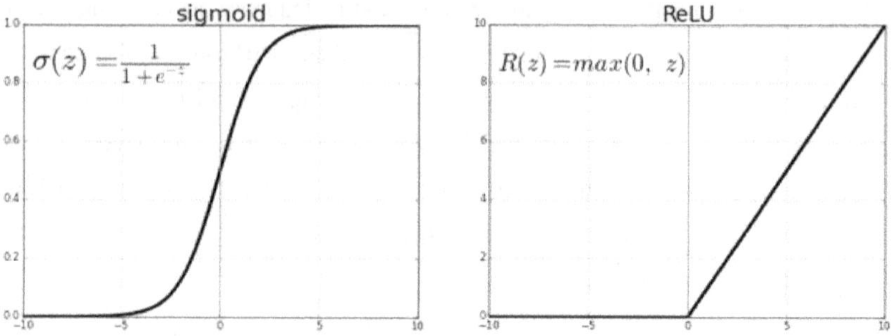

Fig. 1.3 Activation Function of CNN

Pooling Layer: Layered computing comes after array computing, taking into account the five-person pooled restriction.

$$Q_i = max(p_i1, p_i2, \ldots, p_in) \tag{1.3}$$

Array computation is followed by layered computation with the five-person pooling constraint in mind (Figure 1.4).

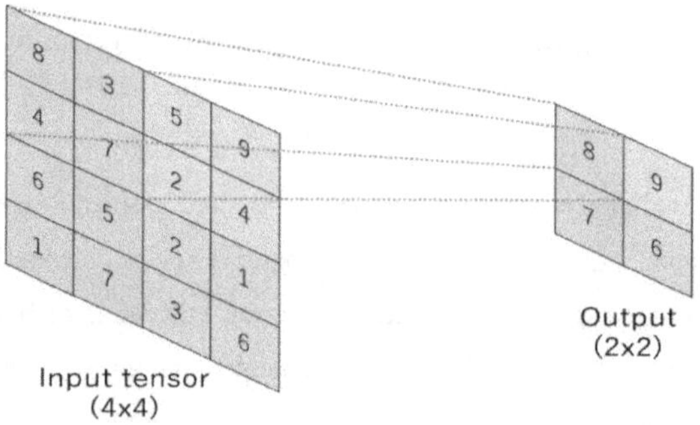

Fig. 1.4 Max Pooling Layer of CNN

1.4.2 Recurrent Neural Network (RNN)

RNNs are a type of neural network designed to handle sequential data, making them particularly useful in applications such as time-series forecasting, Natural Language Processing (NLP), and anomaly detection in IoT systems. The traditional neural networks process each input independently. The RNN used a feedback mechanism that allows data from previous steps to predict the future outcome. This capability makes effective for tasks that required the recognition of patterns such as speech recognition, machine translation, and network security. The RNN model contain the recurrent cell that maintains a hidden state based on the input data and previous state (Das et al. 2023).

$$h_t = f(W_h h_{t-1} + W_x x_t + b) \quad (1.4)$$

Where h_t shows the hidden state at time t, x_t is the input at that step, W_h and W_x are weight values, b is the bias, and $f$is an activation function such as tanh or ReLU. This structure shows the RNN to remember past data and used it in for future inputs as shown in Figure 1.5.

The standard RNN model raises the issues such as vanishing and exploding gradients, which hinder their ability to capture long-term dependencies. To addressed the using the advanced models like Long Short-Term Memory (LSTM) and Gated Recurrent Units (GRU) were utilized. The LSTM model contains the memory cells and gated mechanisms that regulate the flow of data and relevant data is retained over extended sequences. The GRU is a simplified version of LSTM by combined the forget and input gates into a single update, reduced the computational complexity that maintain the efficiency.

The RNN is a tool in intrusion detection for IoT networks to select the patterns in sequential network traffic for detecting cyber threats. The RNN extensively used in predictive analytics that help to forecast sensor data in smart grids and enhance security in blockchain-integrated networks. The RNN-based models contribute significantly to improve the real-time anomaly detection, and decision-making in complex IoT environments.

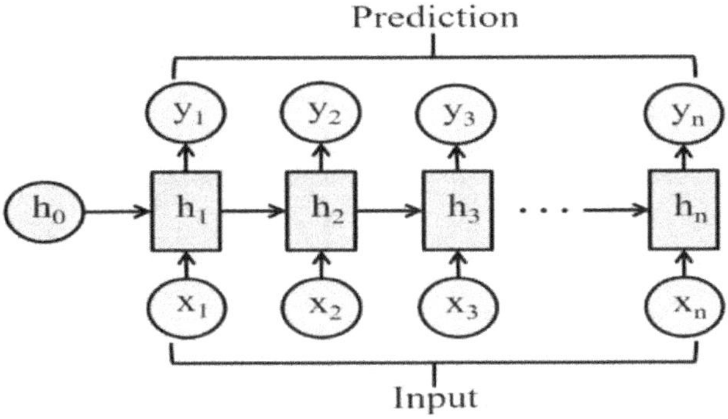

Fig. 1.5 Fully Connected RNN (Mienye et al. 2024)

Two fundamental types are needed by contemporary IDS: Anomaly-based Intrusion Detection System (AIDS) methods and Signature-driven Intrusion Detection System (SIDS) methods. The fundamental concept of SIDS is comparing the digital signature of the present activity with a collection of earlier recorded attack patterns; whenever both sets of data match, an alarm will be raised. An entirely novel attack which is incompatible with no previously discovered characteristic in the record set is therefore extremely unlikely to be detected by the SIDS approach. Consequently, the SIDS approach is unable to stop future attacks.

This represents the main problem with the plan and its biggest weakness. In the area of AIDS, ML techniques have developed a framework for the typical actions for an automated system. An incursion is any significant departure from the predicted behavior that occurs among the system and reality. To ascertain the possibility that additional attacks have taken place, the data does not need to be updated frequently, compared to the SIDS approach. A particular ML technique, including the SVM, the K-Nearest Neighbors (KNN) or DT, forms the foundation for several investigators' theories regarding the presence of AIDS.

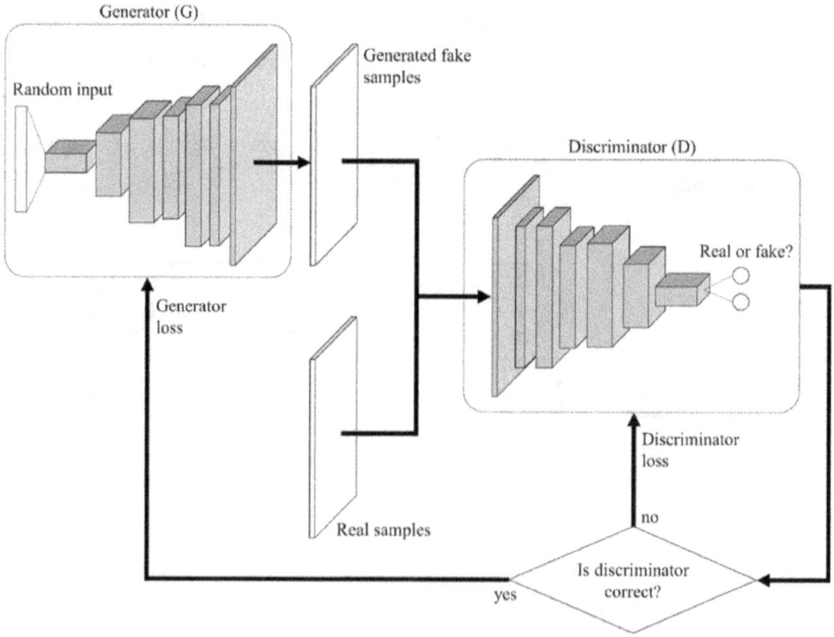

Fig. 1.6 Typical Architecture of GAN (Alqahtani et al. 2023)

The DT classifier takes a lot of time, especially throughout its training stage, whereas the SVM and KNN models have trouble with poor and huge quantities of data. Even though NB fast generating rate renders it inappropriate for real-time data consumption, this investigation also suggests adopting it (Kitsune et al. 2018). The web's and telecommunications technology's explosive growth has drastically changed a few fields, particularly network protection (Yisroel et al. 2018).

A network's infrastructure along with every of its facilities linked to the internet can be safeguarded by a number different safety policies, including IDS, antivirus programs, and antivirus program. These tactics defend networks against attacks that come coming from within and beyond an organization. Unfortunately, a significant portion of IDS still produce an unusually high volume of false alerts.

Whenever adequate training information is provided, the IDS can attain high sensitivity levels and ML models that are adequately stretched to detect attacks. Additionally, ML is an attractive alternative since it is easy to create and develop and doesn't demand specialist knowledge (Dawit et al. 2020). Conventional IDS and system management's efforts were inadequate for identifying any aberrant or fraudulent activity (large information) because the IoT is essentially a huge network containing huge quantities of data (Dawit et al. 2020).

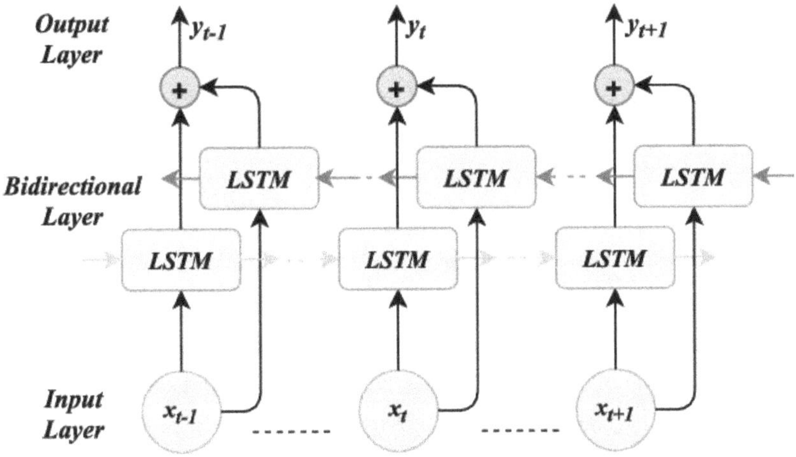

Fig. 1.7 Typical Architecture of BiLSTM (Pavlatos et al. 2023)

In an IoT network, this project will implement IDS that are both host-centred and networking-based. The type of IDS is determined by the positioning of sensor clusters. The sensors, also known as agents, in any Host-based Intrusion Detection System (HIDS) system gather information about malicious activity. Network Intrusion Detection System (NIDS) examines hosts and routers, analyzes network traffic, and generates log reports or alarms if it discovers suspicious nodes. SIDS infrastructure, currently no longer in use, were influenced by antivirus software. This application looks for unusual activity from malware or byte patterns in network traffic.

It makes choices by analyzing receiving data using the databases it maintains. On the other hand, AIDS techniques keep a watch on network activity and alert users to unusual data. Keep in mind that sensor nodes have restricted assets when developing a monitoring system for connected objects. Consequently, due to the NIDS architecture can function both the host machine or gateway stage (Saldamli et al. 2020).

1.4.3 Deep Blockchain Approach for Anomaly Detection in Bitcoin Network

In various industries, anomalies—also known as behaviors or observations—that deviate from commonly anticipated or typical data present a challenge. "An abnormality identification" refers to the process of identifying and separating these anomalies. The goal of the sophisticated process known called One-Class Categorization (OCC) is to precisely find observations that exhibit activity that differs from the norm.

The core of anomaly finding is its ability to identify unusual values, abnormalities, or variations in the data which could usually go undetected by conventional analysis techniques. The capacity to identify anomalies is increasingly important in today's data-rich environment for preserving the dependability and integrity of networks, whether in the medical care, financial, the field of industries. The idea behind identifying anomalies is that most data points follow a predetermined standard or normal behavior (Calikus et al. 2025). When defining something is deemed "normal" a framework or system can comb through massive datasets to find instances that do not fit the Mold. This sophisticated method is especially helpful when abnormalities are generally uncommon but have significant implications. In computer security, for instance, the identification of unusual patterns can signal a possible a computer virus, but in healthcare, it might draw attention to rare patient circumstances that require immediate attention.

The OCC highlights the fundamental challenges of identifying anomalies problem, which is to train a model with a huge amount of standard information to identify abnormalities without providing a precise definition of exactly what constitutes an anomaly. The intricacy of identifying anomalies and the need for sophisticated methods that can adjust to emerging trends and distinct outliers are reflected in its unstructured aspect.

To put it simply, the identification of anomalies is an important tool for uncovering hidden perspectives, preserving system resilience, and improving the general calibre of decision-making procedures. Mahdavifar et al. (2019) suggested ever-changing environment, maintaining the confidentiality of data-driven infrastructure, reducing risks, and remaining informed of future dangers all depend on the advancement of identifying anomalies algorithms.

1.5 Blockchain Technology

In the last two decade the blockchain technology become a significant advancement with the ability to completely change a number of different professions. The blockchain represents a distributed, decentralized record platform for transactions. Blockchain uses a network of computers called nodes, as opposed to conventional centralized records, to verify and preserve transactions in an unchangeable way (Difrancesco et al., 2023). Blockchain offers an useful and affordable option for a variety of applications because of its distributed method, which increases trust, increases security, and does away with the requirement for brokers.

The potential of blockchain system to offer secure records serves as one of its main benefits. The blockchain transactions are secured, time-tagged and connected to earlier transactions, guaranteeing data security and protecting against unwanted changes (Nguyen et al., 2022). The blockchain is especially useful in sectors in which precise and safe record is essential in finance, medical services, and logistics and supply chain planning. All network users' access to the identical verified data, the transparency provided by Blockchain increases user credibility.

Blockchain usage is steadily increasing as businesses realize how it may improve operational security, efficiency, and transparency (Joshua et al., 2018).

1.5.1 Features of Blockchain

The number of advantages given by blockchain architecture is a desirable option for safe and effective transfer process. The following features shows the safety and increased working during operations, support its broad acceptance across organizations.

Integrity: The potential of blockchain to protect the accuracy of data is one of its key features. All the registered users are able to access activities that are stored on an online ledger, providing integrity and visibility. The Blockchain works on a consensus process, whereas changes can simply do if all trustworthy individuals agree Jia et al. (2025). The remote verification mechanism protects the accuracy of collected data, by reducing the illegal activity and improper data.

Increased Privacy: Blockchain enhances privacy using robust cryptographic techniques to protect sensitive data. The traditional centralized systems data is stored in a single location and is vulnerable to breaches. The blockchain contains the distributes data across multiple nodes (Idrees et al. 2021). Each transaction is encrypted and linked to previous transactions and make unauthorized access to difficult. The participants can control the level of information that share only authorized entities can access specific data.

Enhanced Traceability and Recognition: The blockchain improve the accuracy and visibility used to maintain the constant record of the all transactions. The organization of the supply chain management that track the movement of items. The organization track the product's entire lifecycle, production to delivery using blockchain technology and reduce the risk of fraud and illegal products. (Chen et al. 2019).

Secure and Productive Transactions: Traditional transaction processing methods include longer verification processes, agents, and individual authorization, can cause delays and failures. By automating transactions with smart contracts self-executing contracts with specified guidelines the blockchain reduces such obstacles (Bhumichai et al., 2024). Without the need for agents, this technology ensures smooth execution, speeds up transaction processing, and lowers human error. Thus, companies are able to function more effectively and complete transactions instantly.

Cost-Effectiveness: The accessibility of blockchain system is one of its primary benefits. The traditional business and financial transactions usually have the third-party agents like money transfer companies or banks, which increase processing time and expenses. By allowing direct peer-to-peer transactions, blockchain reduces the need for these agents (Bhumichai et al., 2024). Since there are a few third parties involved, transaction fees and management costs are reduced, making Blockchain an affordable option for both consumers and companies.

Security and Fraud Prevention: With a rise in illegal activities and cyber risks, security is an important issue in the digital era. Blockchain's decentralized and protected features reduce these dangers. While hash functions are used to record all the transaction, it is generally difficult to change previous data without a network consensus (Hussan et al., 2019). Also, the use of distributed ledger technology reduces the possibility of centralized attacks and unauthorized manipulations, it verifies that no single entity controls the entire system.

Decentralization and Trust: Blockchain runs on an independent network, in comparison with standard centralized systems where data is controlled by an individual organization. By reducing the necessity for a central authority, this decentralized system boosts user trust. Transactions can be fully verified by users, ensuring system fairness and transparency. As there is no single point of failure, the remote structure also improves system strength, making Blockchain more durable to operational errors and cyber threats Zhang et al. (2019). Blockchain technology, which gives better safety, accuracy, and transparency, is changing the management of transactions and data. Blockchain is being utilized in many different businesses to reduce risks and improve procedures due to its cost-effective operations, global architecture, and encrypted security features. Applications for the technology will increase as it develops further, giving us new options for safe and effective online transactions (Farren et al., 2016). Organizations and industries must stay ahead of these advancements to leverage Blockchain's full potential and drive innovation in their respective fields.

1.6 Related Technologies of Blockchain

Distributed Ledger Technology (DLT): This technology plays a big role in commerce by recording information on ownership discernibility, assessment, financial transactions, and other things. The traditional approach has also relied heavily on data. Information have shifted from conventional formats to more sophisticated structures because of the widespread usage of computing devices and digitized Kumar et al. (2021). Similarly, under the simple electronic system, data have been authorized and maintained by external parties. The proposed method encourages the collaborative development of digital paperwork that have the capabilities and attributes of being created and modified by multiple parties.
In essence, a dispersion recorded is an information source which may be distributed across many geographical locations, structures, and enterprises. Every individual within company has an identical duplicating value for the data. All copies within the specified time frame reflect any updates or modifications to the data. Utilizing encrypted computations, such as sophisticated markings and hashing features, data is maintained and accurate Neelakandan et al. (2022).

A common structure known as a commitment was used to define the instruction for establishing or changing the evidence. Criteria such as whoever is entitled to what is recorded in the standard ledger will be included inside of this contract.

Effective Agreement: Effective agreement is defined as the multiparty computation that enables share grasping in the form of an agreement between several partners without the need for any complex meetings or third parties to mediate the transaction Salim et al. (2021). It is a contract in which the terms agreement among the buyer and the seller are expressed as an element of software that runs in accordance with the re-characterized requirements.

To put it simply, the contract is the self-executable program which is followed, performed, and ordered based on agreements and criteria reached by at least two parties. The magnificent agreements were used to reapply and then execute the distributed records. The entire Blockchain architecture relies solely on clever contracts to implement company logic on the shared Ferrag et al. (2021).

1.7 Blockchain Applications

Ethereum provides a freely available Blockchain framework that supports distributed applications and intelligent agreements. Intelligent agreements, or autonomous agreements containing encoded concepts, were first provided by Ethereum. Some Ethereum Virtual Machine (EVM) agreements run periodically when specific conditions are satisfied. Ethereum represents the native coin. Participants who perform network computing and authentication are compensated. It also powers smart contracts. Distributed programs that operate on a distributed ledger system instead of a server, are permitted on Ethereum (Nguyen et al. 2022). This includes applications in gaming, social media, and finance, such as bitcoin exchanges. Ethereum 2.0 is moving away from Proof of Work (PoW) and toward Proof of Stake (PoS). The objectives of this improvement are cost-effectiveness, protection, and sustainability.

Ethereum 2.0: Ethereum is currently undergoing through several stages of a significant update known as Ethereum 2.0 (ETH 2.0). The ability to scale and efficiency of the Ethereum infrastructure are enhanced by this update. Ethereum represents one of the top platforms for distributed banking that includes trades, financing, and financing with no the need for middlemen.

Initial Coin Offerings (ICOs): A lot of organizations acquired money by releasing Ethereum Blockchain coins throughout the ICO craze.

The network of distributed ledgers is another name for Blockchain software. It might appear to be an accumulation of physically connected information due to its title. Each block contains a crypto encode, transactional information, and the time of the transaction. The DLT uses encrypted hashes to link chunks. This conceptual sequence begins with the origin block shown in Figure 1.8. The Blockchain is unique, distributed, and uncopiable. We will talk about diversity and the Byzantine issue. Distributed agreement is suggested by the Blockchain. Abnormal Magnetic Resonance Imaging (MRI) images could indicate malignant tumors. Abnormal fingerprinting use of technology could be a sign of an illegal attempt to enter a secure area without authorization. Abnormal payments using credit card information may be a sign of criminal activity, which could point to a questionable attempt to enter a secure location without authorization.

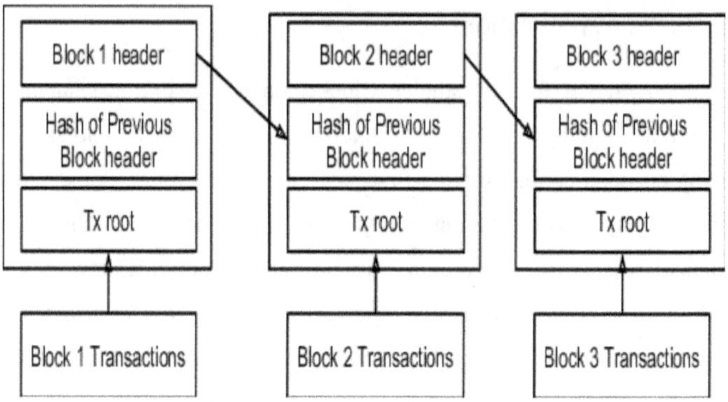

Fig. 1.8 Structure of Blockchain (Joshi et al. 2018)

Hash Graph: In the realm of decentralized ledgers, the Blockchain method is currently increasing popularity. Nevertheless, the concept of Blockchain contains several built-in drawbacks. POW, a form of consensus covered in the section on "Blockchain protocols" in this section, is used by several organizations. As previously stated, the lengthy PoW procedure results from the Blockchain's ineffective high consumption of power. Hash graphs eliminate transaction authentication by using Directed Acyclic Graphs (DAG) for agreement.

Blockchain Network: In a Blockchain infrastructure, the channel for communication among the different member locations is defined by the system itself. The most frequently utilized peer-to-peer network utilizes conversation; but, as confidentiality concerns increase, semi-gossiping and straight peer-to-peer relationships have been employed. Additionally, the network's size and the protocols that control it are explained, clarifying the system's role as an open ledger platform. There are three applications for a decentralized ledger. As an example, the limitations are as follows.

The General Public: A state-of-the-art publicly accessible Blockchain serves as one which is constructed with freely available software and requires no authorization. While entering the network, individuals do not have to get permission from the authorities.

There is an advantage of the mechanism of consensus by downloading a binary or the source files, installing the application remotely on their Personal Computer (PC), and then starting to validate activities that are published to the community. Each network member can analyze and select new chain segments by utilizing this recent improvement.

Collaboration: Specialized organizations led by entrepreneurs oversee collaboration a distributed ledger There are leaders in groups. Internet users cannot join or validate operations on Blockchains that are private. The Blockchain can be made public, restricted, or hybridized by companies that grant the authority to read it.
Because of their scaling, velocity, and financial confidentiality, group Blockchains are being used in many industries. Collaborative-developed Blockchains are utilized by companies that collaborate through "decentralized" consortium Blockchains (Jia et al. 2025). For many businesses, Blockchain technology is enhancing business processes. It is used in managing supply chains, the financial sector, and medical. The Blockchains developed by the Consortium include R3 The Corda network, Quorum, which and Hyperledger's.

Private: A single entity develops, oversees, and owns proprietary block chains. Different parties create, manage, and preserve accessible Blockchains. Access privileges may be restricted, public, or a combination of both. In this limited setting, external public assessments are required to maintain the framework's legitimacy. Blockchain innovation is used within secured Blockchains, however the solving issues techniques are kept confidential (Idrees et al. 2021). The concentration of private Blockchains could jeopardize privacy. Verified credentials and approved system participants are advantageous to encrypted Blockchains. These benefits come from organization.

1.8 Relevance of Blockchain, Machine Learning, and Deep Learning

Decentralized Trust: IoT sensors can function in a thrustless setting by utilizing Blockchain technology. By removing primary places of weakness and improving protection, every device might autonomously validate activities and data.

Effective IoT Agreements: Blockchain technology can enable effective agreements that run autonomously in response to predetermined triggers. This could result in safe, self-regulating behaviors for IoT that utilize information entered from several devices.

Fraud Identification: ML can assist in spotting odd trends and alerting users to possible security risks or device issues due to the enormous volume of interactions and information points collected through IoT systems.

Preventive maintenance minimizes delay and possible damage by using DL strategies to evaluate information collected by corporate IoT sources and forecast when tools may break down or need replacement.

1.8.1 Unambiguous Blockchain Agreement

The three agreement procedures that Blockchains use are described here.

PoW: Participants in the Network must use PoW to confirm that merely authentic activities have occurred and discard any that appear to be malicious. Members are rewarded when authorized activities have been added to block and the distributed record. Computation speed mostly affects the PoW system. Finding the absence hash is a competition between multiple network points. The bitcoin recipient is determined by the hash value. This hash is the result of a difficult computational endeavour due to the customizable nature of the ledger.

PoS: The purpose of verification of threat, a proof-of-stake substitute for proof-of-work, was to prevent computing races throughout the validation phase. A group of terminals is capable of being produced by cooperative members of a network's evidence of concept protocol. Members may extract blocks and get prizes faster as a result. Consequently, this network pool's bandwidth usage increases, and the infrastructure shifts to a less structure. To choose a participant who will be verified in the following block, Verification of Stake uses a selection procedure.

Proof of Authority (PoA): Employing a voting process, this method, which is becoming more popular in the realm of confidential digital currencies, verifies blocks. Voting to determine if an operation needs to be accepted as authentic and added to the existing chain is done by a group of well-known and reliable nodes. Compared with PoW, these contribute to increased throughput and a decrease in the period needed for validation. This agreement strategy is supported by an extensive number of sectors due to its authority for mechanism permissions. Navigate, decisions provided by authorized user centers need to be constantly immune to external intervention to accomplish full decentralized.

While DoS and disruptive breaches reduce connectivity, data replaying attacks safeguard network stability. The variety of attacks produces weaknesses in present protective measures which cannot be reliably minimized, rendering it hard to avoid every intrusion and uncover all anomalies in VANETs. As a result, identifying anomalies is challenging. According to Chen et al. (2019), proactive network safety solutions are therefore crucial.

Protection of Blockchain: It is based on the idea individuals need to be prepared to confidentially exchange crucial data, particularly since they distrust one another. This is the foundation of distributed ledger activities. Because of the complex decentralized database and agreement procedures, intruders will need assistance to influence the framework. Community connections are maintained and confidential data is protected by cryptography. Blockchain computing tries to resolve the complicated contract. However, the event of a failure, it guarantees network reliability.

Decentralized Governance: There are several hazards associated with central databases. Peer-to-peer transmission of information on Blockchain lowers this possibility. Peer-to-peer networks lack a central data centre, making it difficult to gain access to vulnerabilities. Additionally, it removes vulnerabilities that can cause the entire network to fail. Networking node secrecy on the distributed ledger is made possible by crypto public-private credentials that enable all communications. Networking nodes are protected in this way. Bitcoin is incredibly safe because it uses private and public keys to securely store and decode data. The Journal of Economics (2015) asserts that digital ledger records are essentially unchangeable. When information becomes distributed, each network member receives the same treatment.

Byzantine Conundrum: A Byzantine challenge occurs when devices in a distributed network display disparate data. Therefore, it is necessary to tackle a Byzantine challenge in an increasingly central manner.

The nodes in the chain are not trustworthy. The situation is hard to confirm whether their data was received. Think about attempting to reach a consensus among a distributed network of terminals while a small portion of them is flawed and could launch a breach on the entire network. Addressing the Byzantine problem requires a comprehension of this. In agreement, Byzantine endpoints have the potential to deceive and contaminate additional nodes. The bitcoin network needs to work consistently and come to an agreement despite having many byzantine nodes.

Bitcoin: This template was used by Bitcoins. They created a technique that stops someone from changing times or time signatures on documents. Merkle trees allowed documents to be consolidated into one block and enhanced organizational effectiveness.

Nevertheless, the distributed ledger has been assigned to Nakamoto. The initial Blockchain-based system resulted from approach. Bitcoin represents an exchange of peer-to-peer payments. Its name comes from its distributed ledger architecture. Bitcoin is a crypto-currency. Bitcoin's special characteristics allow it to function as digital currency. As a result, network trades are documented in a publicly accessible ledger. Unanticipated problems may arise with digital copies of products. Bitcoin is currently under development to address a few important problems (Jia et al. 2025).

The initial need is that the electronic representation cannot be technologically replicated. Since an electronic asset's owner may become confused if it is copied. Furthermore, the framework becomes unreliable when the replicated resource is used repeatedly. The exact position is described by the double spend dilemma. PoW is used by Cryptocurrency to get around this problem.

To verify transactions for a portion of freshly created bitcoins, mining employs proof-of-work. Threats that take advantage of flaws in equipment or firmware might result in unanticipated performance errors. When the number of real-time embedded equipment increases, such assaults increasingly plausible and accessible. An embedded system attack can result in a fatal diabetes medication overdosing or disable a car's brake mechanism.

For monitoring techniques to produce useful findings, flaws and attacks must be found promptly and accurately. Atypical behavior is unable to remedied when it is discovered incorrectly, and failing may result from a late correction. Threats and organization breakdowns are like disease that affect the entire system. It is essential to identify the signs of a medical condition, keep an eye out for themselves, and act quickly if some are discovered to save an entire system from going down (Hassan et al. 2019). Knowledge keeps illnesses from harming organizations. During every trade, the buyers and sellers might create new identities to conceal their actual identity.

With its various uses, identifying anomalies remains one of the most challenging problems to tackle. Concepts differ by civilization and situation and are frequently imprecise. Events that are out of the usual are called anomaly. However, abnormal event identification is hard due to dependent on context interpretations. Cryptocurrency transfers include several factors. However, according to the manner they are carried out, customer or transaction actions are capable of being categorized.

Transactional situations and likely harmful behavior are examined in this thesis. Due to the complexity associated with Blockchain operations, this concept sheds light on Cryptocurrency statistical analysis. To provide light on Bitcoin research, this study examines financial information. Transactions recorded on the digital currency Blockchain become more complex. The two primary categories of abnormalities are regional and worldwide (Zhang et al. 2019). The researchers discovered that there are issues with authenticity, safety, confidentiality, and credibility in decentralized IoT-driven intelligent cities. The proposed structure has multiple levels for three components: two for credibility alongside a single for confidentiality. Reliability is managed using a Blockchain-based credibility unit. It protects the infrastructure.

1.8.2 Principal Component Analysis (PCA) and Enhanced Proof of Work (ePoW) are used within Two-Layered Security Components

These components reduce and restructure data to avoid contamination (Farren et al. 2016). The study looks for abnormalities in the distributed ledger data framework. The system's data arrangement can be used in several approaches for searching for anomalies. The digital currency, an asset on the Blockchain, is used in the research. Research data and information are easily accessible. Consequently, this choice was selected. Crypto currency data about transactions undergoes extensive pre-processing to prevent money laundering, fraudulent transactions, and scams. These financial transactions are then found using a variety of modelling techniques.

A comprehensive assessment is conducted following the comparison of multiple algorithms to determine which is particularly reliable. Compared to earlier studies, the present research employs a more thorough approach to identify anomalies in Blockchain information. Crypto currency abnormality analysis becomes possible by fusing state-of-the-art ML with graph concept as its framework.

Digital Criminal Activity: Over the past few decades, there has been a notable rise in fraud via the internet. By the present, cybercriminals might reach $2.3 trillion. According to the

Northwest Denver Information on in 2015, credit card forgery caused the United States $1.4 billion. A report published in 2016 by the European Federal Bank found that the cost of a credit or debit card theft is one euro for every 2,595 euros invested. Economic scams, neither the threat of cyber terrorism online extortion, cyberspace, or e-terrorism, is the main topic of the present research.

Banking is the primary focus of hackers. Many computer security vulnerabilities as well as hacks are caused by system-level flaws. The risk of some risks has been significantly increased using Blockchain. Due to internal constraints and administration, many financial organizations are keen to automate. In each year there are significant loss of money. An example of a common fraudulent transaction is stealing credit cards. This conduct is worldwide. Even though AI aids in the detection of illegal credit card operation, numerous criminals continue to evade detection. An estimated 45 million payment card records were impacted by the Adobe Technologies assault. Identities, purchase histories, dates of expiry, and encoded credit card information are retrieved. After gathering credit card details from 1,720 South African cards, a 100-individual collaboration stole 14.7 million Dollars from 1,400 businesses in a single afternoon. They left Tokyo when the crime was reported to the government.

Blockchain technologies improves the security and anonymity of financial systems. This structures, while was supposed to be unbeatable, has been tricked by outsiders. Most cybercriminals wish to carry out their activities in secret. To accomplish this, hackers must hide their activities or persuade the equipment which their actions are approved. Underreporting occurs for minor or severe cases. But some folks are attention-getters. The initial commercial Blockchain, the digital currency, had been challenged numerous times. Since bitcoin becomes a particularly well-known digital currencies, these issues arise.

1.9 Blockchain-based Security Framework in IoT Environment

The IoT is a transformative technology that enables seamless connectivity and automation across various domains such as healthcare, smart cities, industrial automation, and transportation. However, due to its distributed nature and resource-constrained devices, IoT is highly vulnerable to security threats such as data breaches, unauthorized access, and cyberattacks. The block chain presents a useful technique to improve security in IoT settings.

1.9.1 Challenges in IoT Security

IoT environments consists of number of safety issues.

- **Centralized Security Models:** The conventional security system is easily attacked using DDoS attacks and act as a single point of failure based on dependence on centralized model
- **Data Integrity and Privacy:** The data integrity and privacy in industries like healthcare and finance to data collected by IoT network original and protected.
- **Device Authentication and Access Control:** These challenges indicate the identity of all the devices that make the networks of IoT devices.
- **Scalability and Performance:** A security solution is accessible without affect the performance due to the increase amount of IoT devices.
- **Energy Efficiency:** Traditional methods were ineffective on IoT devices and limited processing and battery performance.

1.9.2 Blockchain-based Security Framework

Blockchain's key features decentralization, durability, and consensus mechanisms—are used by a Blockchain-based security structure in an IoT system for better security. The following features build the overall framework:

Distributed Identity Management

- The IoT devices allows the register in a public record and blockchain reduces need for centralized identity sources.
- Each device in IoT network is unique encryption identity to reduce the risk of intrusion.

Safe Data Storage and Transmission

- The huge amounts of data generate the IoT devices that shared via cryptographic methods and stored in a distributed records based on blockchain.
- Smart contracts stop unnecessary changes and maintain the data integrity.

Consensus Mechanisms for Trust

- Blockchain networks uses algorithms such as PoW, PoS, or Practical Byzantine Fault Tolerance (PBFT) to validate transactions.
- The IoT network used the lightweight mechanisms like Delegated Proof of Stake (DPoS) to optimize performance and energy efficiency.

Autonomous Safety Policies with Smart Contracts

- Self-implementing security mechanism manages execution verification, access control, and authentication using smart contracts.
- The contracts increase efficiency and lower cost.

Distributed Identification and Access Control

- Blockchain uses cryptographic techniques to specific access control systems.
- Blockchain used to automatically generate the permissions for role-based and attribute-based access control.

Anomaly and Threat Detection

- The IDS used blockchain mechanism that safely store attack patterns and monitor the network activity.
- The blockchain used AI and ML models to identify errors.

1.9.3 Advantages of Blockchain-based IoT Security

- **Decentralization:** This reduces the dependency on access points and points of failure.
- **Immutability:** Data cannot be changed after it has been collected and maintain its accuracy and reliability.
- **Transparency:** Improves accountability by enabling auditable transactions.
- **Cyberattack resilience:** Prevents common attacks that include Man-in-the-Middle (MITM) and DDoS attacks.
- **Flexibility and Scalability:** The blockchain properly manage a wide range of IoT devices.

1.10 Motivation

The data generation in IoT network has increased day by day due to spread of IoT devices that causing serious issues with safety, confidentiality, and computational efficiency. The IoT sensor devices are still susceptible to security risks because of their low computing power and storage capacity and difficult to carry out complex security tasks. The centralized information systems and other traditional security measures are expensive, ineffective, and very vulnerable to data thefts. There is an increased demand for strong, decentralized security mechanisms. The seriousness of issues has been brought to light by a number of actual cyberattacks against healthcare IoT networks. For example, if the hospital operations have been affected by ransomware attacks like which target interconnected medical facilities and result in delayed medical services and reduced security of patients. In other reported cases, hackers have taken advantage of flaws in cardiac devices and remote insulin devices to manipulate dose settings and device functionality without authorization. The sensitive health records are also public due to data thefts utilizing networked surveillance equipment, which violates patient privacy and legal compliance obligations. The examples show that IoT devices used in healthcare settings are especially susceptible to significant cyber threats are frequently limited in terms of memory, computing power, and energy consumption.

The blockchain technology gives the significant solution and worked under decentralized, unchanged records that eliminates the need for a central authority to data integrity and security. The authentication of each IoT node is possible to prevent the unauthorized access using blockchain technique. The use of blockchain in IoT healthcare that prevent the patient data and maintain the privacy. This study investigates the Ethereum-based Blockchain model with ZKP authentication to improve the privacy and secure communication between IoT devices.

1.11 Problem Statement

The rapidly development of IoT in healthcare that enables the continuous patient monitoring, remote diagnostics, real-time clinical decision support, and intelligent medical services. The IoT-based healthcare systems used the wearable sensors, medical devices, gateways, and cloud platforms to collect and process sensitive physiological patient data.

The large-scale implementation of IoT system in healthcare presents the security, privacy, and performance issue that directly effect on patient safety and reliability.

The IoT-based health care system is extremely vulnerable from a safety and privacy standpoint due to IoT devices are scattered, diverse and limited in resources. There is an vital symptoms, medical records, and diagnosis data are sensitive healthcare data that needs security and integrity. Many IoT healthcare devices are vulnerable to threats because of lack the processing capability to use robust crypto measures. The single points of weakness are introduced by central cloud-based healthcare infrastructures, raise the possibility of significant data thefts and illegal data manipulation.

The IoT-based health care system generates the enormous amounts of real-time data that need to be processed, and examined with the minimum amount of time from an efficiency and scalable standpoint. The traditional IoT communication designs' heavy reliance on centralized servers causes network congestion, higher latency, excessive energy consumption, and decreased Quality of Service (QoS). These restrictions are particularly important in healthcare settings and inadequate or delayed data have detrimental therapeutic effects.

A number of traditional approaches were addressed the security issue in IoT network. In order to protect IoT medical data, centralized security measures such as cloud-based identification servers and conventional encryption methods are frequently employed. The traditional IDS of rule-based or signature-based methods are used to identify hostile activity. The traditional methods have serious drawbacks, such as high false alarm rates, low scalability, excessive computing overhead, and the incapacity to identify threats.

The ML and DL-IDS techniques investigated recently to increase detection accuracy. The traditional models suffer from overfitting, restricted generalization, imbalanced datasets, and high training cost. The majority of IDS methods are made as stand-alone parts and are not closely linked with communication protocols, safe storage, or authentication systems and unable to offer an all-encompassing security measure for IoT in healthcare

The absence of distributed security and data transmission model represents another significant research need. The blockchain technology was presented as a possible decentralized authentication solution, current blockchain-based IoT systems have inadequate privacy protection, significant latency, and high energy usage. Some existing studies are inappropriate for use in healthcare applications because they rely on public blockchain transactions that reveal private information. Moreover, not enough research has been done on how to combine effective low-power communication protocols using blockchain security features.

- The IoT consists of collection of interconnected devices called as nodes that enables to obtained and transfer the data across the device. The rise of IoT connectivity has resulted in a large number of linked devices and the sharing of data among them which effect on user confidentiality.
- The two main issues with IoT represent security and privacy is the fundamental IoT constraints.
- Internet and IoT-connected devices have limited processing power and that need an affordable and efficient security framework.
- Existing IoT Architectures need to re-design keeping these points in considerations.

1.12 Research Objectives

- Analyze different security challenges in the existing architecture of Internet of Things.
- Apply different methodologies for managing secure access to and exchanging data from IoT devices.
- Develop new design of secure architecture for IoT applications.
- Compare the performance of proposed architecture with exiting architecture.

1.13 Significance of the Study

This study has significant contribution to the secure deployment of IoT-HCS by proposing a unified model that addresses security, privacy, intrusion detection, and communication efficiency. The proposed model works on the decentralized, privacy-preserved devices verification and tamper-resistant data management based on the integration of the Ethereum-based blockchain with ZKP authentication mechanism. The proposed hybrid At-GAN-BiLSTM intrusion detection model enhance the ability to detect complex pattern and cyber threats with reduced false alarm rates. The optimized LoRaWAN–MQTT communication model improves scalability, latency, and packet delivery performance and suitable for large-scale and real-time healthcare applications. This research advances the existing approach to offer the comprehensive and scalable security solution to the unique constraints of healthcare IoT environments.

1.14 Study Limitations

The performance of proposed model is measured using simulation and benchmark datasets that are not fully captured the variability and unpredictability of real-world healthcare environments. The blockchain implementation focused on an Ethereum-based network and performance of model may vary when deployed on alternative blockchain. The DL–based intrusion detection model needs the sufficient labeled data for effective training which is critical issue to obtain in practical healthcare data. Another is resource constraints of low-power IoT devices also limit on-device deployment of complex learning models that required the high edge or gateway-level processing.

1.15 Research Scope

The main scope of this research is to design and measure the performance of a secure and scalable IoT model for healthcare applications. The model worked on decentralized security system based on blockchain and IPFS and detect the intrusion using DL techniques and also communication through LoRaWAN–MQTT integration. The proposed model is validated in healthcare-centric scenarios and also proposed models are generic and adapted to other IoT domains such as smart grids and industrial automation. However, aspects such as large-scale real-world deployment, regulatory compliance analysis, and hardware-level optimization are beyond the scope of this study and are identified as potential directions for future research.

1.16 Key Contribution of the Work

This research presents two innovative security models for IoT-HCS, addressing major cyber security challenges while ensuring efficient data transmission and real-time threat detection. The key contributions are as follows:

Model 1: Blockchain-Assisted DL for IoT-Based HCS

- **Hybrid At-GAN-BiLSTM IDS:** The study proposes an advanced DL model that combine the GAN with BiLSTM model that apply the attention mechanism to enhance attack detection in IoT network. This model improves detection accuracy and reduced the False Positives rate.

- **Blockchain-Based Security model:** The Ethereum-based Blockchain model is proposed that combined the ZKP authentication to provide tamper-resistant data storage and prevent unauthorized access to sensitive patient information.
- **Decentralized Data Storage Using IPFS:** The IPFS secure and decentralized data storage, and addressed the challenges related to data integrity, scalability, and tamper resistance.
- **Experimental Validation on Benchmark Datasets:** The model obtained accuracy of 99.9% on CICIDS-2018 (D1) and 99.1% on ToN-IoT (D2) that indicate performed well as compared to the traditional intrusion detection models.

Model 2: LoRaWAN-MQTT for Secure IoT Data Transmission

- **Development of a LoRaWAN-MQTT Model:** The model presents the improved LoRaWAN framework that combined to the P/S MQTT protocol and provide the facilitate efficient and secure data transmission in IoT network.
- **Optimization of Network Performance:** The proposed model reduces the network congestion, improves PDR, and optimizes message transmission delay using the P/S mechanism for smart grid and industrial automation applications.
- **Scalability and Adaptability in Large-Scale IoT Deployments:** The proposed model is designed for IoT applications such as medical care, smart cities, and monitoring system to reliable and secure communication across diverse organizations.
- **Experimental Performance Evaluation:** The proposed LoRaWAN-MQTT model show the significant improvements in data transmission, reduce the latency and maintain the high reliability and security in large-scale IoT networks.

The integration of blockchain security mechanisms with DL-based intrusion detection and optimize the IoT communication protocols based on the LoRaWAN-MQTT. This study presents approach to enhance the security, efficiency, and scalability of IoT-based system and related applications.

1.17 Organization of the Thesis

Chapter 1: This chapter discusses in detail the IoT and its applications, blockchain technology, intrusion detection and cyber security methodologies, blockchain-based security framework in IoT environments, and challenges in IoT security. The problem definition and investigation summary are also presented in this chapter, which also covers components and attack detection systems.

Chapter 2: This chapter discusses the combined use of several cutting-edge methods, such as the IoT, blockchain, and DL, with particular concentration on DL in healthcare IDS, and NIDS is the main topic of this chapter. These methods' confluence creates an extensive platform for improving handling data and security measures based on Blockchain in IoT.

Chapter 3: This chapter presents the complete methodology of the research over the different security threats that occur in IoT environments. This chapter discusses the two proposed models based on blockchain to transmit the data securely over the IoT environment and proposes an enhanced LoRaWAN with MQTT model for secure data transmission in IoT environments for intelligent grid systems.

Chapter 4: This chapter presented the result analysis of the proposed models and measured the performance using the several evaluation parameters. This chapter also compares the proposed models' results with the existing state-of-the-art or existing methods.

Chapter 5: This chapter concludes the overall research work and presents the future direction of this study.

CHAPTER 2

Literature Review

2.1 Overview

The widespread use of interconnected devices over major fields including healthcare, intelligent grids, manufacturing automation, and highways has been made possible by the Internet of Things' rapid expansion. The IoT networks increase productivity and automation but they face significant safety, confidentiality, and functionality issues due to its distributed architecture, resource limitations, and diversity. The IoT platforms have been increasingly targeted by malicious actors such botnets, virus transmission, theft of information, and sophisticated persistent threats in recent years, especially in healthcare settings where access to data and sensitivities are critical.

Investigators have investigated a variety of security measures using IDS, ML and DL models, blockchain-driven trust models and improved communication protocols and to solve the issues. The current solutions frequently concentrate on discrete security and performance concerns and fall short of offering a comprehensive, scalable, and secure architecture. This chapter addresses the research needs that drive the suggested models by reviewing earlier studies in IoT security, blockchain-powered model intrusion detection approaches, and effectiveness of evaluation strategies.

2.2 Theoretical Framework

Three basic principles form the theoretical basis of IoT security investigation: accessibility, privacy, and integrity. Cloud-based authorization, encryption, and access control systems are the foundation of conventional centrally managed security approaches. These methods, however, fail to adapt with large-scale IoT implementations and present single points of fault.

A decentralized trust model is brought about by the blockchain system and data integrity and transparency are improved via distributed agreement, consistency, and cryptographic authentication. The blockchain provides a strong basis for safe IoT devices when paired with privacy-preserving techniques like ZKP and distributed storage solutions like IPFS.

The learning intricate attack trends from internet traffic and system performance of ML and DL-IDSs simultaneously offer adaptive and data-based protection. In order to identify abnormalities, botnets, and malware in IoT and blockchain networks, complex models including CNNs, LSTMs, GANs, transformers, and hybrid models were extensively investigated. Next-generation IoT security model was theoretically based on DL-based identification of threats and blockchain-based trust management.

2.3 Security Challenges in the IoT

In addition to device diversity, constrained processing resources, and constant data flow, IoT systems provide a number of security problems. The unauthorized access, identity theft, data manipulation, surveillance, and DDoS attacks are typical dangers. Large-scale IoT botnets have shown how hacked devices can be used as weapons to carry out destructive cyberattacks.

The sensitivity of medical data and the need for immediate availability make these issues more severe in the healthcare IoT. Due to changing attack tactics and dynamic traffic patterns, conventional firewalls and signature-based intrusion detection systems are frequently useless. Furthermore, unified protection is challenging due to the lack of defined security standards among IoT devices.

The lack of generalisation in ML-based IDS models, which causes detection accuracy to drastically decline when classifiers undergo validation on untested datasets or actual traffic, is another key problem. This is a challenging task that designed the adaptive, scalable, and domain-informed security mechanisms.

2.4 Security Models, Frameworks, and Methodologies for IoT

Several safety mechanisms including blockchain, machine learning, and deep learning were presented to improve IoT protection. The secure data exchange, tamper-proof logging, and decentralized authorization are the main features of blockchain-based security solutions. The Blockchain-driven medical communication architectures and studies like the confidence-Worthy Privacy Preservation Secure Framework (TP2SF) show increased confidence and integrity, although they frequently have scalability issues and substantial computational costs.

This research observed that a botnet, also known as an Internet of Things botnet, is a collection of connected gadgets, web-based devices, and other internet-connected devices that attackers have compromised and are using maliciously. Typically, a botnet consists of computers set up to surreptitiously monitor other devices over the website from a distance without the owners' consent. Additionally, the creators of the workstations have made them able to forward emails to different computers connected to a shared network over the global internet. Several existing models focus on secure data transmission based on the different models:

Kumar et al. (2021) suggested the TP2SF model for smart cities that contain three key components: a trust model, a two-level privacy mechanism, and an intrusion detection model. The two-level privacy mechanism integrates ePoW with PCA for secure data transformation. The intrusion detection model used optimized eXtreme Gradient Boosting to identify and respond to security threats in real-time. The performance model was measured across ToN-IoT and BoT-IoT datasets to improved detection rate.

Neelakandan et al. (2022) developed the Blockchain with DL-based BDL-SMDTD model to secure medical data transmission and disease diagnosis. The model captures the medical images, and the encrypt using Moth-Flame Optimization-Elliptic Curve Cryptography and stored on a blockchain to enhance security. The model used image processing techniques and Inception and ResNet-v2 model for feature extraction and an SVM for classification. The model obtained an accuracy score 96.94%.

Salim et al. (2021) proposed a model movement pattern in channel state data gathered from multiple receivers to differentiate users from attackers. A profile-based model was implemented to prevent identity theft attacks. The Handover Authentication model reduced FAR. The DL-based LSTM model was used to prevent attacks from legitimate users. The model obtained the accuracy of 0.91 on healthcare data.

Ferrag et al. (2021) suggested a Federated DL model that combined the RNN, CNN, and DNN model for cybersecurity in IoT environments. The study evaluates the performance of federated DL in enhancing IoT security. The performance of both centralized and FL models was analyzed using three benchmark datasets: Bot-IoT, MQTTset, and ToN-IoT. The final results shows that FL-based DL models outperformed non-FL models that indicate the superior attack detection accuracy.

Hanna et al. 2021, Praveen et al. 2021 suggested the various communication techniques. For instance, the authors of Seoane et al. (2021) and Wytrebowicz et al. (2021) measured the commonly used protocols such as Advanced Message Queuing Protocol

(AMQP), Hypertext Transfer Protocol (HTTP), Constrained Application Protocol (CoAP), and MQTT based on factors such as resource consumption, message overhead, latency, and reliability. The MQTT shows the most suitable protocol for IoT networks due to its efficiency and also gained popularity in industrial automation, transportation, and smart grid application in facilitating control signal transmission through traditional CNN models.

Another study suggested by (Chenning et al. 2023, Ould et al. 2021) based on several protocols for the data and Media Access Control (MAC) layers. The LoRa is utilized due to widely application of Low Power Wide Area Network (LPWAN) and its scalability, coverage, and resilience. (Almuhaya et al. 2022) presents issues related to bandwidth, latency, and throughput. The previous studies were analyzed LoRa physical and LoRaWAN efficiency and not considered its application in a P/S model by (Idris et al. 2022, Navarro-Ortiz et al., 2022).

The several researchers were developed a P/S model that combined with LoRaWAN and measured the performance using delay, frequency, and adaptability to similarity with other protocols. This model is among the first to assess MQTT under LoRaWAN within the Network Simulator 3 (NS-3) simulator, that includes several core IoT routing protocols. The study provides insights into the performance of the P/S model in LoRaWAN, enabling other researchers to optimize configurations based on specific requirements. Notably, the study does not introduce novel methodologies but rather examines MQTT performance within LoRaWAN.

The IoT represents a collection of associated electronic objects with IP addresses and the capacity to send data, such as electromechanical sensors, automobiles, commercial and home electronics, and pacemaker-placed surveillance systems. Abdulkarem et al. (2021) referred to them as objects in the context of the IoT. An investigation for the California-based business safety firm Evidence found at the very end of the year 2013 which a botnet comprising digital televisions, cooling systems, and other types of household gadgets, in addition to desktop machines, was the origin of millions of fraudulent emails. While observing that certain emails were forwarded via an authentication gateway, an investigator learned the details.

Desktop computers that have been unlawfully taken by a botnet are referred to as bots. The phrase "something bot" was created by Evidence employee David Knight to describe any technological device which is not a typical computer. After learning the Deep Recurrent Neural Network (DRNN) and Long Short-Term Memory Autoencoder - Deep Recurrent Neural Network (LS-DRNN) algorithms on the Bot-data set, the investigators assessed how well they performed. The processes in the investigation's strategy, "data preparation," "simulation" and "model assessments," was presented by Li et al. (2017).

The authors also suggested the innovative model that used the supervised learning strategies to identify risks. The model also identifies the patterns to issues by models that utilize selected features through the runtime of intelligent. The final outcome of predictive models performed well as compared to the conventional static analysis tools to detect security problems and obtained the significant accuracy (Smith et al. (2020).

Johnson et al. (2021) categorize security challenges into several key areas, including consensus techniques, digital contracts, infrastructure of networks, and privacy concerns. Authors discuss common vulnerabilities including 51% attacks, fraud, and problems with electronic contracts, as well as a number of preventative measures like encryption techniques, improved agreed protocols, and formal authentication methods. The study also highlights new advancements and possible avenues for security Blockchain research, emphasizing the need for ongoing innovation and adaptation to counter evolving threats.

Doe et al. (2019) investigate two significant security vulnerabilities in Bitcoin smart contracts: re-entry and quantitative overload. The investigators present a detailed analysis of security flaws might be exploited, citing real-world incidents such as the DAO attack for re-entry that cybercriminals repeatedly triggered a scheme to obtain funds. Additionally, they talk about numeric overflowed which occurs when mathematical operations go beyond variable bounds and produce strange results. The report offers a thorough analysis of current prevention and identification methods along with suggestions for enhancements for enhancing automated contract security. The researchers show how well their suggested fixes work to stop these attacks using demonstrations and empirical assessments.

A comparative summary of different available IoT data transfer, security, and communication techniques across application domain, techniques/models, and key limitations is given in Table 2.1.

Table 2.1: Summary of IoT Data Transfer, Security, and Communication Techniques

Author / Ref.	Application Domain	Techniques / Models Used	Key Contributions	Limitations Identified
Kumar et al. (2021)	Smart cities	TP2SF framework, ePoW, PCA, XGBoost	Secure data transmission with trust modeling, privacy preservation, and intrusion detection	High computational time
Neelakandan et al. (2022)	Healthcare IoT	Blockchain, MFO-ECC, Inception, ResNet-v2, SVM	Secure medical data transmission and disease diagnosis	Limited generalizability
Salim et al. (2021)	IoT authentication	Channel State Information, LSTM, Ho-Auth	Secure handover authentication and identity theft prevention	High latency
Ferrag et al. (2021)	IoT cybersecurity	Federated DL (CNN, RNN, DNN)	Improved attack detection accuracy using FL-based DL models	Data imbalance issue
Seoane et al. (2021), Wytrębowicz et al. (2021)	IoT communication protocols	MQTT, CoAP, HTTP, AMQP	Comparative evaluation of protocols; MQTT shown as efficient	Security overhead not fully addressed
Chenning et al. (2023)	LPWAN IoT	LoRa, ZigBee, LTE	Scalable and low-power IoT communication	Limited bandwidth, latency, and throughput

Almuhaya et al. (2022)	LoRaWAN evaluation	Simulation-based performance analysis	Identification of LoRaWAN efficiency constraints	No publish–subscribe architecture
Navarro-Ortiz et al. (2022)	Publish–subscribe IoT	MQTT over LoRaWAN	Evaluation of MQTT performance under LPWAN	No novel optimization techniques
Li et al. (2017)	Botnet detection	DRNN, SDRNN, LS-DRNN	Accurate botnet detection using supervised learning	High dependency on dataset quality
Smith et al. (2020)	Blockchain security	ML-based smart contract analysis	Effective detection of vulnerabilities in smart contracts	Focused on limited attack types
Johnson et al. (2021)	Blockchain security	Survey-based analysis	Classification of blockchain security threats and solutions	Lacks experimental validation
Doe et al. (2019)	Smart contracts	Vulnerability analysis	In-depth study of re-entrancy and overflow attacks	No automated detection framework

2.5 An IDS for Cloud Infrastructure and Malware Protection that uses ML-based Blockchain

The advances in ML, rapidly growing data development, and the most recent technological and communication advancements made it possible to solve simple to complicated issues like breaches into databases. Networks and their information can be protected using ML-based Intelligence IDS systems.

Combining Blockchain as well as structural technological advances, Mantripragada et al. (2024) presented a high-security way for transmitting medical records. This structure included the collecting of health data and the use of the built Whale Optimization – Deep Belief Network (WO-DBN) to confirm the node's harmful nature. After the fraudulent nodes were eliminated, healthcare data were transmitted via not harmful nodes. Blockchain-based technology was used for encryption of these medical photos to secure their transfer. The DL model was used to diagnose the disease based on these conveyed data. The performance of the suggested DL model was 1.66% higher than that of other DL models obtained from dataset-1 when this suggested medical data transfer and illness diagnostic infrastructure was analyzed (Murthy et al. 2024).

The Ant Lion Optimization alongside Hybrid Deep Learning (ALOHDL) model is employed in the Bitcoin Supported IoT Medical System presented by Alamro et al. (2023). IoT gadgets used in hospitals may safely transfer healthcare information to the Block-Hash Signature - Ant Lion Optimization alongside Hybrid Deep Learning (BHS-ALOHDL) technology, which also identifies network attacks. The ALO-based feature subset choosing mechanism is used in the BHS-ALOHDL approach to generate several vectors of characteristics. For surveillance, the HDL framework combines LSTM and CNN features. Finally, the HDL strategy's ideal a tuned hyperparameter is accomplished by utilizing the flower pollinating algorithms which is its identification rate.

Mozumder et al. (2024) introduce a new DL-based powered by Blockchain cryptography framework for safe healthcare information handling. The idea under discussion includes a variety of stages of operations, such as encoding, optimal key creation, and secured handling of information through Ethereum. By giving hospital administrators read/write permission and initiating preventive contracts, it gives people the power to control the availability of data. Employing a block-cipher approach, suggested method provides a dependable way to generate secure encryption keys and successfully protect critical healthcare data. The average person can make certain patient data is kept private and safe from unwanted access by using this technique. Utilizing healthcare data is used to carry out the detecting technique.

To achieve protection suggested by Rajeshkumar et al. (2023) addresses designing medical services using BC technologies. The Intelligent Medical Organization System with Blockchain-Assisted Security Assessment and Information Aggregation. Utilizing a deep stacked sparse autoencoder framework and spiralling optimization of searches, the proposed approach first detects intrusions. Additionally, the proposed model uses a $softmax$ in conjunction with EfficientNet to extract features for the categorization of medical images. Through applying the SPO approach to optimize the proposed approach's hyperparameters as the threat detection performance of the proposed technique was increased. Numerous empirical evaluations can be carried out to show how the framework has improved, and the results are examined using various metrics. The thorough comparison analysis highlighted how well the proposed approach performed in contrast to alternative methods.

The Blockchain-based secure health care platform using DL techniques suggested by nature inspired over the IoT network was proposed by Singh et al. (2023). The investigation's initial phase presents a Blockchain-based safe information retention framework, authorization of users, and medical condition forecasting. Following min-max standardization of information, dwarf mongoose optimization is utilized for extracting features and selections. The enhanced bumblebee mating optimization approach with Bi-LSTM is employed to categorize the medical condition into two distinct categories. The unusual data are stored in the corresponding individual Blockchain for the time being. The use of Blockchain serves to securely keep healthcare information for future research. The precision rate, encoding, and decryption period of the proposed model are evaluated by comparing it with various baseline approaches. The suggested techniques accomplish a certain amount of protection.

The investigation by Almalki et al. (2024) focused on determining how Blockchain is used in cutting-edge medical facilities that are enabled by FL. The combined utilization of Blockchain alongside intrusion identification monitoring has become advantageous for identifying and avoid fraudulent activity throughout the repository nodes. ML techniques are used to assess data collected at a common data storage location to identify illnesses and enable healthcare providers to recommend the right treatment. The framework of this research focused on how these models can be used effectively for medical management. Reaching 94 % effectiveness for evaluating diseases and dependence is made feasible by the combination of FL along with the suggested framework.

Employing the cryptographic techniques RSA (Rivest, Shamir, Adleman), SATDO (Self-Adaptive Tasmanian Devil Optimization) for most effective keys, SHA3-512 (Secure Hash Algorithm 3 - 512 bits), and an Intrusion identification Mechanism for identifying risks in IoT network, Alserhani et al. (2024) shows an authentication management assessment for IoT nodes alongside routing information. The suggested method aims to improve IoT system cybersecurity by confirming the reliability and legitimacy of information transferred across nodes and detecting and blocking network attacks. The suggested TDO procedure serves to create keys effectively, the RSA approach is used to secure the stored information, while the SHA3-512 method was used to ensure data security. The suggested DNNs are used to identify Intrusions. The AOA serves for optimizing the DNN. The programming language Python is used for simulating the constructed model, and the outcomes are assessed and contrasted with those of alternative models that are currently in use. The results show that the design is effective in detecting and thwarting attacks simultaneously offering safe and dependable connectivity in IoT-enabled, contemporary, intelligent vertically networking.

During the last decade, IDS utilized Nearest Neighbors (NN), DT, Naive Bayes (NB), and SVM classifying techniques. The most challenging parts of using these techniques are choosing the optimum detection characteristics and modifying the algorithm's configurations (Bernal et al. 2019). Each approach has disadvantages. Classification algorithms can use optimal strategies to get across these obstacles.

Rauniyar et al. (2021) state that data recognition and processing are essential to building an attack identification platform. Normal and unforeseen activities can be distinguished by the platform. The goal of this study is to improve the dataset model. This study enhances intrusion identification systems. The suggested model ought to be implemented more quickly in this work than the SIDS intrusion identification method. Numerous tried-and-true feature extraction techniques are used in this investigation to enhance processing speed and data accuracy. The effectiveness of RF, DNN and one-R models was evaluated in this investigation using 10-fold cross-validation. The CICIDS-2017 dataset was utilized in this research to assess computational approaches. This study shows that the proposed classifier works better than the signature-based intrusion identification method in both intrusion identification and alarm-related mitigation. It also establishes a network of IoT devices. An intruder identification program is installed on the Blynk host. Several risks are present on the internet long prior to and once the intrusion recognition mechanism is turned on. They consist of DDoS assaults and port examinations.

An intrusion identification and categorization model using ML was created by Jaradat et. al. (2022). The data set must be structured for the model to work. It will then have a variety of appealing features. KoNstanz Information MinEr (KNIME) then used classifiers for processing the modified data set. Three different classification methods were selected for this study to enhance performance and comparative analysis used the CICIDS 2017 dataset and the KNIME Analytical Framework to evaluate predicted algorithms. Classification algorithms are compared in this article according to their primary uses. In comparison to previous methods, the tests demonstrated an effective performance rate of 98%. Investigators studying information analysis and cyber safety are encouraged by this work to use ML to build intrusion identification techniques that have become more effective.

Majeed et al. (2021) investigated the potential benefits of using a Web of Things for connecting and conversing with sensors via the internet. As a device develops, its complexities, dimensions, performance, and flexibility all increase. According to this article, the Web of Things (WoT) controls the globe and affects people's lives with its many services and activities. Sinkhole assaults, overhanging drops, and administrative assaults can happen even with WoT's wide range of applications. The WoT has no defense. Comparable attacks that compromise the safety of an organization are identified by the interruption paradigm.

There is a lot of company expense and latency within the most common centrally cloud-based attack identification platform. As a result, attacks and the detection of unauthorized users take time (Abdullah et al. 2021). According to Darley et al. (2022), a tremendous quantity of data is produced by thousands of sensors worldwide. Every phase of collecting information, transfer, preparation, transportation, and storing makes it vulnerable. ML is being used by some scholars to find basic behavioral trends in data. Data gets better. This offers real-time confidentiality and security prevention and identifies anomalies in the framework. Certain problems can be addressed by a variety of ML techniques. They are capable of successfully managing confidentiality and protection. ML outperforms earlier methods in intrusion identification by identifying attack tendencies. The existing research on ML for identifying intrusions is reviewed in this study. The current investigation examined scholarly papers from two distinct databases between 2010 and 2022 using PRISMA. The results of the ultimate studies showed that ML could be used in malicious attacks from systems by increasing the difficulty, energy consumption using data pre-processing, necessary extracting features, ML model learning, and the implementation of ML-based surveillance systems.

Attack detection is defined by Kumari et al. (2022) includes any effort to jeopardize the functioning, protection, or functionality of an organization. IDSs find weaknesses and anomalies in network cybersecurity. The process for detecting intrusions has improved in the past few decades. Regarding claims because it is relatively soon and inadequate as a comprehensive security solution, this sector has expanded quickly. Network and safety managers give priority to this duty. Therefore, it is capable of being augmented by ever more secure technologies. IDSs can forecast upcoming incursions based on historical ones thanks to data extraction for malware identification. The available research on data mining techniques for IDS is examined in this study. This strategy involves data extraction techniques for standard and real-time identification of intrusions.

According to Papadopoulos et al. (2021) assault area grows quickly as new devices and capabilities are added to the worldwide web. Profit is taking precedence above security and confidentiality in the IoT sector. Identifying suspected or unidentified intruders is not anymore possible using standard defense systems. Intrusion detecting methods using ML have accurately detected threats that were earlier unidentified. ML models can be attacked in several ways. Prior to deployment, adversarial cases can be used to verify the robustness of the model. Instances of aggressive behavior from the real world are necessary to create an aggressive framework. The suggested strategy is dominated by two approaches. A model is tricked into incorrectly classifying data by label infection. The quick gradient signature technique, another choice, evades identification. Analysis demonstrates that an adversary can alter data or avoid identification.

According to Layeghy et al. (2022) might not be applicable to networks in the actual world. This study tested the ability to generalize of ML-based NIDSs by applying seven ML techniques to four recently published standard NIDS datasets. No frameworks that are generalizable across every data set were discovered by this investigation. Significant generalization imbalance is shown in this information. This implies that detection performance could be greatly increased by moving categorizing from the original system to the targeted system.

The findings imply that under the examined circumstances, supervised learning models generalize in comparison to ML techniques. As shown by SHapley Additive exPlanations (SHAP) values, there cannot be a strong link among any number of attribute values and the Attack/Benign categories in a single dataset-model coupling when such relationship exists across different samples with distinct feature patterns. This relationship is unique to this dataset-model combo. This demonstrates that a dataset-model combine lacks generalization when there is a substantial correlation among several parameters and the Attack/Benign categories.

According to Tahri et. al (2022), the World Wide Web has altered the course of history. When participants require assistance, it connects them to others in their community and assists them in maintaining their relationships on social media. It oversees several web pages as well. People and businesses are at danger when they share both private and professional data. The data is always at danger due to its reliance on the World Wide Web. IDS shields users of the World Wide Web from dangerous network intrusions. IDS system alerts network supervisors when it detects suspicious activity in network traffic. The optimal method from the initial phase is used in the subsequent phase of processing the record set. The researchers utilized both datasets to validate the model. To verify the efficacy of the suggested strategy, researchers conducted tests on the Network Security Laboratory – Knowledge Discovery in Databases (NSL-KDD) and University of New South Wales - Network Based 15 (UNSW-NB15) datasets.

Riyadh et al. (2021) argued that increasing amount of computer systems that are linked together, an outbreak is defined primarily a rise in online information transfer. Due to its intricacy, routers and antivirus programs are unable to identify harmful activity in such information. Therefore, to safeguard the accessibility and reliability of data, system administrators need to identify hostile behavior. This proposes building an intruder identification platform to address data difficulties by utilizing a KNN algorithm and clustering feature concepts. Comprehensive, hybrid, and distorted information all have problems. These issues are addressed by this technique, which provides several identical pattern metrics. As a result, the suggested approach is effective. The proposed method performs better even when identification accuracy declines. This is still the case considering that the proposed strategy employs SVMs, although with a reduced prediction effectiveness.

As demonstrated by Mohsin et al. (2021), system expansion has become crucial in modern society, and privacy of information is a significant scholarly issue. Networked sensors and activities are monitored by IDS. Although contemporary surveillance systems have observed new attacks, decreased false alarms, and enhanced identification efficiency, flaws still exist. To tackle the mentioned issues, numerous researchers have created Machine Learning-based Intrusion Detection Systems (ML-IDSs). All most fundamental distinctions across ordinary and excellent information can be discerned by computers. You can accomplish this by yourself. Because ML becomes generalizable, it can identify threats that are not yet understood. Leveraging data object's crucial aspects as the organizational concept, this work attempts to develop an IDS classification that arranges and condenses the existing research on DL-based IDS. Researchers base their choices on the assumption that scholars studying online activity protection can apply this classification.

Using a ML network-based IDS to secure networks was recommended by Mondal et al. (2022). To find hostile challenges, their equipment classifies network traffic. Look through the content of the package. Eight classification techniques were assessed in this investigation as model substitutes. The best classification results are obtained with DT and RF. Several models are compared and discussed as an outcome. In accordance with Garg et al. (2021), an intelligence-based IDS may examine the infrastructure and application of the network and assess a botnet attack. The system may alert administrator when identifying the invader. During the previous IDS have entered the professional market.

However, the main shortcomings of current IDSs include alarms that are false, low accuracy, and smaller chances to identify new attacks. Investigators have tried a variety of ML techniques to address the problems. These methods reliably differentiate between typical and abnormal network traffic flows or user information. The investigation evaluates and categorizes ML techniques suitable for IDS. Additionally, they go over individual technique's parameters and measurements. The UNSW-NB15 dataset, that depends on real internet traffic and numerous ML techniques, is used in an empirical investigation (Seraphim et al. 2018).

According to Apruzzese et al. (2022), network NIDS are challenging to develop using the supervised ML. Data needs to clearly differentiate between normal and fraudulent samples to develop and validate Machine Learning-Network Intrusion Detection System (ML-NIDS). Because labelling requires costly expertise, operations are hindered and authors are forced to use out-of-date data. In subsequent, the scenario is improving with tasks providing their tagged data.

Unfortunately, most previous efforts only used these information sets simply "still more" testing facility, utterly ignoring the numerous potentials that their accessibility offered. Researchers resisted ML-NIDS by using already labeled data. Although this strategy has not received significant attention yet, it requires careful consideration from trained experts due to its complexities. Researchers created the initial cross-evaluation approach as a direct result of this. This model demonstrates how cross-evaluations might uncover novel aspects of advanced neural data extraction and ML approaches in practical application scenarios. It may be able to function with tagging. Such comparisons and investigations, yet, present serious difficulties. They created an initial structure for accurate cross-evaluations using system flow (Alothman et al. 2018).

Chen et al. (2020) suggested the Blockchain techniques that enhance the privacy of IoT frameworks. The researchers discussed a number of IoT-specific security concerns, such as permission, secure connections, or data confidentiality. Investigators investigate the issues resolved by Blockchain's distributed and immutable record features. Blockchain-enabled IoT cybersecurity solutions were broken down into a number of aspects such as identity handling, private data protection, and authentication and authorization and also examines the integration challenges and efficiency problems of deploying Blockchain in Internet of Things environments.

Zhou et al. (2021) suggested the number of ML techniques to identify the attacks in IoT network. The suggested ML models identify the security threats in IoT situations. Authors also addressed the challenges posed by IoT systems, such as device variability and resource constraints. The study examines existing IDS and proposes a framework that uses hybrid ML techniques to improve detection efficacy and reduce mistake rates. The investigators also highlight areas that require more research to analysis and scalable methods for widespread IoT deployments.

Yang et al. (2020) suggested the distributed model based on the blockchain technology and address a number of IoT security challenges such as privacy concerns, unauthorized access, and data tampering. The suggested model is blockchain-based security features for the Internet of Things and provide access control, data accuracy, and secure identity on centralized authority. The study demonstrates the practicality and effectiveness of these methods in real-world IoT applications. The investigators also address possible integration problems and suggest future lines of inquiry to enhance usability and efficiency in Blockchain-enabled IoT safety measures.

Table 2.2 gives a brief summary of current ML/DL-based IDS works for cloud infrastructure security and malware defense when combined with blockchain

Table 2.2 Summary of Related Work on IDS for Cloud Infrastructure and Malware Protection that uses ML-based Blockchain

Author and Ref.	Dataset Used	Method Used	Findings	Limitations
Mantripragada et al. (2024)	Brain MRI Images	WO-DBN	Accuracy score of 98%	Might be overfit the model
Hayam et al. (2023)	ToN-IoT and CICIDS-2017	BHS-ALOHDL	Accuracy score of 98%	Requires extensive hyperparameter tuning
Mozumder et al. (2024)	Edge-IIoTSet	CNN BiLSTM)	Accuracy score of 96.02%	Susceptible to overfitting

Rajeshkumar et al. (2024)	NSL-KDD	Deep Stacked Sparse Autoencoder	Accuracy score of 99.04%	High memory consumption
Singh et al. (2023)	Remote patient data	IBBMO-Bi-LSTM	Accuracy = 98%	Limited generalization on unseen data
Almalki et al. (2024)	NSL-KDD	FL	Accuracy = 97.13%	Communication overhead
Alserhani. et al. (2024)	NF-UQ-NIDS	DNN and Archimedes Optimization Algorithm	Accuracy of 98.94%	Model complexity increases training time
Rauniyar et al. (2021)	CICIDS-2017	RF, DNN	Avg Accuracy of 91%.	Lower accuracy compared to DL approaches

2.6 Deep Blockchain Approach for Anomaly Detection in Bitcoin Network

Several comprehensive investigations were conducted since there is a dearth of freely accessible data on various types of APT attacks in infrastructures. The distinction across network attack identification and APT assault identification could be closed with the use of extensive research. Persisted determined attacks, typical attacks, security scenarios, and system security are all covered in the present piece. Utilizing authorizations, abnormalities, this article summarized several approaches for connected devices.

The combined use of ML approaches alongside suggested hybrid agreement approaches and benefits over identifying anomalies, extracted features, and cyber-attack prediction are shown by Venkatesan et al. (2024). The combination techniques take advantage of and maximize the security, reliability, and credibility of the suggested compromise protocols. Still, to improve security and make intelligent decisions in consensus guidelines, this study also investigates a variety ML approach. use the ProximaX ledger framework to show the effectiveness that the advised approach is in decentralized systems. The investigation shows the suggested architecture is a secure, energy-efficient system that adjusts to changing circumstances. Additionally, it incorporates strong agreement procedures, privacy-enhancing attributes, and ML techniques to identify and stop cybersecurity risks (Venkatesan et al. 2024).

Popoola et al. (2021) created a framework for classifying traffic in DNN networks. FedAvg is used on several edge sensors for maintaining DNN modeling remotely from an algorithm resource server. Predictions become better. A worldwide DNN framework is constructed using certain model variables, including server-edge connectivity phases. The N-BaIoT Bot mimics botnets of zero-day peripheral devices. The results of this study show a Distributed DL architecture prefers FDL to concentrated, dispersed, and Coded Deep Learning (CDL).

According to Atayero et al. (2021) argued that minorities are incorrectly classified using the DRNN framework. An efficient DL technique was developed using the Long-tailed Age Estimation (LAE), Synthetic Minority Over-sampling Technique (SMOTE), and DRNN techniques. The LS-DRNN technique was used. This study uses the Bot-dataset to test the approach. The availability of data capacity was reduced by 87% utilizing LAE. In this investigation, the amount of network traffic characteristics in the test set were decreased from 38 to 12 dimensions.

Abasi et al. (2024) suggests a Transformer-based architecture to deal with issues like the temporal relationships, intricate feature relationships, and class imbalance seen in Bitcoin Transaction (BTX) data. The model's stability and efficiency are increased by capturing complex interactions between transaction variables using self-attention techniques, featured embedded data, and positioning encodings. Extensive tests show that the Transformer design performs better than the others, reaching 99.5%.

Mukhtar et al. (2021) suggested detecting side-channel leaks using DL. It is compatible with edge technologies. Simulations of target-algorithm attacks are necessary for DL. Prior studies assessed edge device security using several ML-based side-channel threat frameworks. Attack models are optimized with the application of quantified. Data synchronization and reducing features were the results from protective edge enhancement investigations. An artificial network-based side-channel assault examination instrument may obtain the peripheral device's hidden key approximately 97% reliability thanks to the deployment of the susceptible approach.

Htwe et al. (2020) investigated the N-Badetection framework using ML. This idea makes use of freely available IDS samples and Classification and Regression Trees (CART) style technologies. Compared to CART, NB has a smaller trial recognition accuracy of 98%. ML-based successive botnet attack identification was suggested by Soe et al. (2020).

Effective feature selection is necessary for detecting systems that are lightweight and high-performing. ML methods include Artificial Neural Networks (ANNs), J48 DT, and NB. 98% of botnet attacks are accurately identified. Several sub-engines for different attacks are included in the proposed design, which also identifies botnet-based cyberattacks. Investigation supports the findings.

Venu et al. (2022) discovered that technologies and networks were becoming more susceptible. Efficient identification of attacks and prevention are necessary in these contexts. Because of security flaws, attackers can compromise devices and build botnets from them. Intruders will use an effective DDoS assault to attack selected domains or operations after breaching and joining a million of gadgets to a botnet. Training samples are a constraint for botnet identification algorithms. Botnet-trained ML fails on other datasets. There are several assault techniques.

The investigation proposed using reliable features for determining botnet assaults. Whatever data set can use this. The proposed feature set outperformed three datasets of learned ML techniques for botnet attacks. The models of botnet attacks have been investigated.

Considering the rise in DDoS, malicious software, and BIDS assaults, Waqas et al. (2021) investigated cyber safety. The multiple ML classifier was used to design the ensemble model. Several devices for sensing and N-Ba samples were used in this study to validate the strategies. Testing of IDS assesses performance and effectiveness. The tree-based method outperformed previous methods employing the identical detectors with an accuracy rate of over 98%.

According to Saeed et al. (2021) effectiveness, and resource-friendly. Numerous evaluation standards were met by the approach. The approach outperformed better than the One-Class SVM developed by Hindy et al. (2020). One-class SVMs are tested towards zero-day malware in the work. Autoencoder encoded and decode are optimized in the finalized version. Crucially, autoencoders detect sophisticated zero-day attacks. NSL-KDD has an accuracy of 90% for zero-day identification, whereas CICIDS2017 gives 97%. This study also looks at choices between memory and ramifications.

Instead of evaluating data stored in cloud servers, Hussein et al. (2022) advised users to do it individually on their handheld devices. TinyML may additionally evaluate low-resource Arduino simulations using ML models. This article summarizes both TinyML concept and studies. Micro-ML frameworks are examined in this work. The research presented here outlines datasets, components, and their distinct characteristics to explain the present situation of current research and project possible future requirements.

Joshi et al. (2022) developed a straightforward, extensible, and flexible framework that can evaluate a single image regardless of its quality. This is performed by 33-nm and CMOS platforms. Ahmed et al. (2022) categorized botnets in real-time. When botnets expand, certain strategies are no longer viable. Botnets are discovered by the current investigation. Bot-IoT was examined by Atayero et al. (2021). The DL method quickly and precisely identifies botnets. The amount of memory was decreased approximately 87% using the LAE technique. There were 10 network communication factors instead of 37 after the training. SMOTE was used to enhance the LS-DRNN minority class categorisation. The total volume of investigations increased by 11%.

Several ML based techniques were compared by Abu et al. (2022). To analyze attack over the N-BaloT-2021 dataset. Both normal and botnet-infected internet activity are included in the dataset. The organization proceeded or driven. Botnet cyberattacks from compromised devices were discovered by Ensemble Learning Model for Botnet Attack Detection (ELBA). Determine whether ELBA is superior by comparing it with comparable technological advances.

A Bat Algorithm (BA) that used local-global optimal inertia weighting to alter swarming bat movement was studied by Alharbi et al. (2021). For BA swarm variation, researchers proposed Gaussian population beginning. The Gaussian distribution performance and local-global optimum performance were essential for effectiveness since they increased investigation following each local search and repetition. The Model parameters and weighting for ten attack botnets and one healthy targeted class were refined in this study using Bayesian optimization. Neural Behavioral Alignment (NBA) traffic data and both favourable and unfavourable categorization were used in the current investigation to investigate the Local-Global best Bat Algorithm for Neural Network (LGBA-NN) approach.

Shafique et al. (2021) investigated storing memory for transmitted network data. DL was reduced. FDL was developed by the Information Security Committee using hyperparameter improvement, memory area reducing, and class balanced. Particularly, classification using the FDL paradigm lowers transmission costs and network delay.

Alkahtani et al. (2021) integrity-preserving ML techniques throughout Blockchain-enabled addressing the issue of maintaining information secrecy when utilizing ML algorithms in distributed networks. Researchers look at several methods, such as asymmetrical integrity, supervised learning, and homomorphic encryption, highlighting additionally their benefits and drawbacks in regards to protecting sensitive data during the training and interpretation phases.

Patel et al. (2020) suggested the method to detect the anomalies in distributed data networks using DL models. The author suggested the CNN and LSTM model to identify unusual pattern to detect malicious or illegal activity in network. The model analyses the transactions within a distributed ledger and detect anomalies with exceptional recall and accuracy score 94.22% to improve the safety and robustness of Blockchain.

Table 2.3 presents an overview of the existing IDS and attack detection using ML/DL models in blockchain-based settings.

Table 2.3 Summary of Related Work on IDS for Deep Blockchain Approach for Anomaly Detection in Bitcoin Network ML-Based Blockchain

Author and Ref.	Dataset Used	Method Used	Findings	Limitations
Popoola et al. (2021)	Bot-IoT and N-BaIoT	DNN	Accuracy of 97.88%	High computational cost
Atayero et al. (2021)	Bot-IoT	DRNN	Accuracy of 99.93	Requires extensive training time
Tabaghsar et al. (2024)	Bitcoin data set collected from Bitcoin Chart site.	SVM	Accuracy rate of 91.11%	Limited scalability for large datasets
Abasi et al. (2024)	BTX data.	Transformer	Accuracy rate 99.5% in anomaly detection.	Requires high processing power
Kumar et al. (2023)	Google BigQuery Bitcoin Blockchain	LSTM	Anomaly detection improves Blockchain security and integrity.	High memory consumption

	Dataset used for analysis.		LSTM and Isolation Forest effectively identify anomalies.	
Mukhtar et al. (2021)	EM leakage traces	ECA+ML	Max accuracy obtained of 75.7%	Lower accuracy compared to DL methods
Htwe et al. (2020)	N-BaIoT	CART	Accuracy of 99%	Limited interpretability of results
Ali et al. (2024)	UNSW-NB15	ANN, CNN, LSTM, RNN	Accuracy of 96.98%	High model complexity
Pérez-Cano et al. (2025)	Bitcoin transactions	Heterogeneous Graph Transformers	Anomaly detection algorithms identify fraudulent activities effectively. Supervised graph methods emphasize data heterogeneity's importance. Accuracy of 93%	Complexity of graph-based models

2.7 Performance Evaluation in Security Models and Frameworks

The measuring the performance of model using several parameters such as accuracy, precision and practical deploy ability in IoT environments. The existing studies commonly used combination of classification-based and network-level parameters to measure intrusion detection accuracy, reliability, and communication efficiency.

2.7.1 Intrusion Detection Performance Metrics

The performance of IDS was measured using classification parameters such as confusion matrix consists of TP, TN, FP, and FN (Muneer et al. 2024).

$$Accuracy = \frac{TP + TN}{TP + TN + FP + FN} \tag{2.1}$$

$$Precision\ (P) = \frac{TP}{TP + FP} \tag{2.2}$$

$$Recall\ (R) = \frac{TP}{TP + FN} \tag{2.3}$$

$$F1 - score = 2 * \frac{P + R}{P + R} \tag{2.4}$$

$$FAR = \frac{FP}{FP + TN} \tag{2.5}$$

2.7.2 Network and Communication Performance Metrics

Beyond detection accuracy, IoT security frameworks must be evaluated in terms of communication efficiency and resource utilization, especially under constrained network conditions (Muneer et al. 2024).

$$PDR = \frac{N_{received}}{N_{sent}} \tag{2.6}$$

$$Latency = \frac{1}{N}\sum_{i=1}^{N}\left(t_{recv}^{(i)} - t_{send}^{(i)}\right) \tag{2.7}$$

Table 2.4 Symbols and Notations in PDR and Latency equations

Symbol	Description
$N_{received}$	Total number of packets received successfully at the destination
N_{sent}	Total number of packets sent by the source node(s)
N	The total packets counted during the measurement
$t_{recv}^{(i)}$	Timestamp when the ith packet is received at the destination
$t_{send}^{(i)}$	Timestamp when the ith packet is transmitted from the source

2.8 Limitations of Existing Performance Evaluations

The security procedures and agreement methods, blockchain-based security model have substantial delay and power costs to improve trust and data integrity. The sophisticated topologies of DL-based IDS models restrict their applicability for implementation on IoT devices with limited resources due to significant training and interpretation costs (Deepak et al., 2024).

The lot of current research ignores system-wide performance metrics such as communication latency, flexibility, and energy economy in favor of detection accuracy (Kumar et al. 2021). According to Seoane et al. (2021), performance evaluation is often carried out in conventional settings with little regard for a variety of implementation circumstances such as urban, rural, and hybrid settings.

2.9 Summary

The IoT represents an innovation that makes it possible for seamless connection and digitization in a number of fields, such as transportation, intelligent cities, medical care, and automation in factories. The IoT is extremely vulnerable to safety hazards like data theft, illegal access, and intrusions because of its dispersed architecture and limited resources. The blockchain presents a viable way to improve security in Internet of Things settings. This chapter presents and discusses earlier associated research on blockchain-driven security models that improve IoT network security. Future advancements in lightweight blockchain models and consensus mechanisms will further optimize blockchain-based IoT security solutions.

CHAPTER 3
Proposed Methodology

3.1 Overview

The proposed research provides solutions for different security threats occur in IoT architecture. In this study proposed the two models as list below

- Blockchain Enabled IoT based Model for Secure Data Transmission
- To improve the LoRaWAN performance to P/S IoT model to share the data based on middleman for Smart Grid environment

3.2 Proposed Model 1: Blockchain Enabled IoT based Model for Secure Data Transmission

IoT-HCS handles highly sensitive patient data and operates under strict reliability and privacy requirements. Centralized architectures suffer from single-point failures, limited trust, and high attack exposure. Therefore, a blockchain-enabled decentralized framework is adopted to ensure tamper resistance, secure authentication, and data integrity.

To ensure safe transfer of data, this dissertation proposes a paradigm for registering IoT nodes utilizing the DL framework and the Ethereum distributed ledger. In this case, every gadget has a distinct Blockchain identification. Whenever the transmission of data starts, this identification is employed for authentication and verification. The IoT network's reliability is enhanced by this crucial step, which keeps unwanted devices from entering the framework. The suggested method uses zero-knowledge evidence to improve confidentiality and protection. This ZKP allows the platform to examine data without disclosing secret data. This method guarantees that only authorized individuals can confirm the authenticity of the IoT information and protects it from manipulation.

The At-GAN-BiLSTM hybrid DL approach enhances the detection accuracy and categorizes the different types of intrusions by combining an At-GAN using a BiLSTM system. Although the BiLSTM layer analyzes temporal patterns of information to precisely characterize this type of attack, the At-GAN layer has the charge of spotting unusual patterns. Because of its capacity to efficiently capture intricate aspects and dependencies across the data, the At-GAN-BiLSTM model was chosen to identify the attack across the

IoT-based HCS. To detect abnormalities that can point to invasive activities, the BiLSTM feature is especially suitable for analyzing sequential information, including traffic across networks. The At-GAN network with implemented attention strategy enhances the model's ability to focus on the key characteristics of the data, enabling it to spot minute relationships that other approaches would overlook. Furthermore, the GAN feature helps the model learn from the fundamental distribution of typical web traffic, improving its ability to differentiate between fraudulent activity and legal activities. The At-GAN-BiLSTM approach combines these potent methods to offer a reliable and effective intrusion identification approach in IoT-based HCS, protecting private health information and guaranteeing system privacy.

The IPFS is utilized to effectively preserve and disseminate IoT data due to the Blockchain's storage capacity limits. By providing a distributed storage mechanism that can handle massive data volumes, IPFS relieves the Blockchain's storing strain. To ensure availability and adaptability, the data was stored outside of the chain within IPFS, using Blockchain logs serving as identifiers to the actual sources. A DL approach shrinks the data size prior to storage to maximize computational and storage efficiency. By converting the initial information to the lower-dimensional design, this phase reduces the total size of the information set and enables the framework to handle more data before losing its efficacy.

3.2.1 Datasets Description

There are two publicly accessible datasets, CICIDS-2018 (D1) (Alkadi et al. 2020) and ToN-IoT (D2) (Alsaedi et al. 2020), that are used in this research. https://www.kaggle.com/datasets/solarmainframe/ids-intrusion-csv is the link to obtain the D1. Numerous attacks, including brute force, DoS, web attacks, DDoS, infiltration, and botnets, are present across this dataset. The target in the assaulting concept consists of five companies and fifty computers. https://www.kaggle.com/datasets/dhoogla/nftoniot is the link for obtaining the D2. 11 anomalous data sets, including backdoor, Cross-Site Scripting (XSS), scanning, password, DDoS, DoS, normal, MITM, ransomware, and injection, are included in this dataset in addition to one normal data set. Forty-three attributes are labeled, including 1,598,334 "attack" and 79,053 "normal" instances.

- CICIDS-2018 provides realistic, up-to-date attack scenarios closely aligned with real network traffic, making it suitable for evaluating IDS performance in healthcare IoT gateways.

- ToN-IoT captures heterogeneous IoT, edge, and cloud traffic, including modern attacks such as ransomware and MITM, which are critical for validating intrusion detection robustness in IoT-HCS environments.
- The combination of both datasets ensures attack diversity, traffic realism, and generalization capability of the proposed At-GAN-BiLSTM model.

Table 3.1 gives an overview of the important datasets used for intrusion detection and cybersecurity evaluation that are used in IoT and enterprise domains.

Table 3.1 Summary of Deployed Datasets

Dataset	Domain	No. of Features	Attack Types	Normal Instances	Attack Instances
CICIDS-2018	Enterprise / IoT	80+	DDoS, DoS, Botnet, Brute Force, Web Attacks	Large-scale	Multi-class
ToN-IoT	IoT / IIoT	43	Backdoor, MITM, Ransomware, XSS, Injection	79,053	98,334

3.2.2 Proposed Ethereum Blockchain-based HCS

Because of its intrinsic decentralization, openness, and consistency, the Ethereum distributed ledger offers strong cybersecurity benefits when integrated into an IoT-based healthcare organization. These characteristics are essential in healthcare operations to ensure the confidentiality and reliability of confidential patient information sent across IoT endpoints. The suggested method eliminated single points of failure by utilizing Ethereum's decentralized architecture, thereby improving the framework's resistance to attacks. Furthermore, every Ethereum transaction is impenetrable, safeguarding information from unwanted alteration and enhancing stakeholder security. Ethereum's adaptability with a wide range of decentralized apps and networks increases scalability within the multi-stakeholder contexts that are common in the medical field, and it offers dependability while managing critical information related to healthcare.

Alternative Blockchain systems, like Hyperledger, need authorization, while the digital currency has restricted computing powers. Ethereum is suited for a variety of healthcare contexts because it offers both excellent flexibility and safe anonymous accessibility. Furthermore, authenticity of data is made possible by Ethereum's compatible with ZKP while disclosing confidential data. Verification entities can verify the authenticity of information and activities using this encrypted technique without having personal access to the information underneath. Because it preserves privacy requirements while maintaining data integrity, this is a crucial benefit when dealing with confidential data. Considering all things, Ethereum's decentralized design and ZKP compliance serve as the perfect option for a transparent, safe, and impenetrable identification solution.

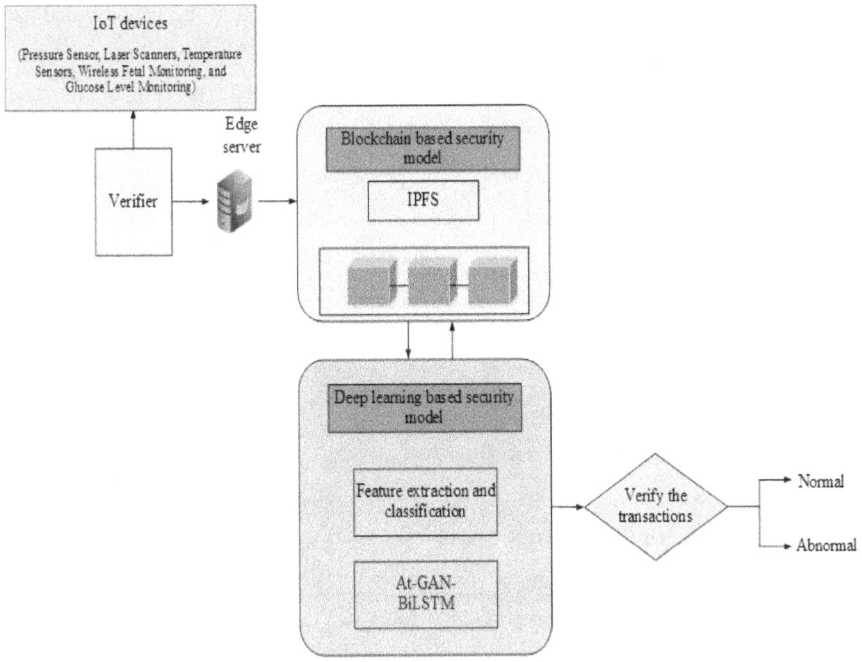

Fig. 3.1 Structure of proposed Ethereum Blockchain-based HCS

The architecture of the proposed Ethereum blockchain–driven healthcare system for secure IoT data transmission is illustrated in Figure 3.1. The proposed architecture integrates IoT devices, edge computing, blockchain technology, and DL-based security mechanisms for privacy and security by design, as well as confidentiality, integrity, and anomaly detection. At the data acquisition layer, the real-time healthcare-related data are collected from various types of IoT devices, including pressure sensors, laser scanners, temperature sensors, wireless fetal monitoring devices, glucose level monitors, and others. Before sending the data, a verification module is used to confirm the legitimacy of the data being transmitted. Once the verification is successful, the data is sent to the edge server as shown in Figure 3.1. The edge server is critical in reducing the communication latency and computational burden at the IoT device level. Security Layer. The Ethereum blockchain-enabled HCS operates in two security layers, which include Ethereum blockchain-based security and DL-based security phase. In the Ethereum blockchain phase, the healthcare data will be validated and transmitted securely using Ethereum smart contracts and IPFS. Where IPFS is used to store large data in a distributed manner, a hash value record is stored in the blockchain. This process ensures data immutability, traceability, and tamper-resistance. In the DL-based security phase, a DL model is used, which is capable of analyzing the pattern of transactions and network traffic. The system uses At-GAN-BiLSTM and the learned transaction pattern to validate the transactions by classifying the transactions as normal or abnormal. This process helps detect the malicious activities at a very early stage. Therefore, the proposed architecture demonstrated in Figure 3.1 shows a hybrid privacy and security model that combines blockchain security and DL-based threat detection mechanisms results in an efficient and scalable privacy-preserving data transmission model for IoT-based healthcare applications.

3.2.3 EBC-based Security Model

The Ethereum Blockchain–based Communication (EBC) security model is designed to provide secure device registration, privacy-preserving authentication, and tamper-resistant data management for IoT-HCS. The model follows a logically ordered sequence of phases of cybersecurity consisting of five phases: (1) Initialization, (2) Registration and Verification, (3) ZKP strategy, (4) Encryption and Decryption, and (5) Creating of Block and Validation.

Table 3.2 Symbols and Notations Used in the EBC-Based Security Model

Symbol	**Description**
S_i	i^{th} IoT device
UID_{si}	Unique Identification Number of device S_i
P_k, Pr_v	Public and private keys of device S_i
BC	Ethereum blockchain network
SC	Smart contract deployed on Ethereum
ZKP	Zero-Knowledge Proof
$H(.)$	Cryptographic hash function
$IPFS$	InterPlanetary File System
Tx	Blockchain transaction
G	Generator point of elliptic curve
r	Random nonce
m	Encrypted healthcare data
W	IoT gateway
NS	Network server

3.2.3.1 Communication Channels and Security Assumptions

Different communication channels are employed at various phases of the EBC model to ensure both security and efficiency:

- Registration Phase: A secure off-chain channel (Transport Layer Security (TLS)/Datagram Transport Layer Security (DTLS)-enabled) is used between the IoT device and the gateway to protect identity credentials during initial registration.
- Verification and Authentication Phase: A blockchain-assisted secure channel is employed, where authentication proofs are exchanged off-chain, while verification results are immutably recorded on the Ethereum blockchain using smart contracts.
- Data Transmission Phase: Encrypted healthcare data is transmitted through standard IoT communication protocols, while hashes of the data are stored on the blockchain and the encrypted payload is stored in IPFS.

This hybrid on-chain/off-chain communication design minimizes blockchain overhead while maintaining strong security guarantees.

The EBC model consists of the following logically ordered phases:

(a) Initialization: The V_e (verifier) is utilized in this initialization phase, the S_i (sensor node) is registered using the V_e. Initially, V_e it chooses the maximum prime number, and it randomly selects the private key $\Pr_v$ and public key PB_v. Then, V_e it selects way cryptographic hash value and optimizes the elements in the network.

(b) Registration and verification: To preserve privacy, authentication is performed using ZKP.

- The device proves ownership of S_i without revealing it.
- The smart contract verifies the ZKP.
- Upon successful verification, the device is granted authenticated status.

In this phase, S_i request them V_e to join the EBC and the V_e registers IoT_i using the given phases:

- The P_k (provisional key) is generated based on the S_i , and it has parameters such as MAC address M_{Si} and the identity sensor ID_{Si}.
- After the generation P_k, the S_i is verified using the Ts_i (timestamp).
- Let Ts_i, M_{Si} and ID_{Si} are transmit to the V_e. The M_{Si} is verified over the black-listed MAC address V_e. if the black-listed MAC is found, the request is terminated. Or else the response is provided to the S_i that P_k is performed correctly. Finally, the PB_v is sent to the S_i for the next process. Figure 3.2 presents the registration and verification stages.

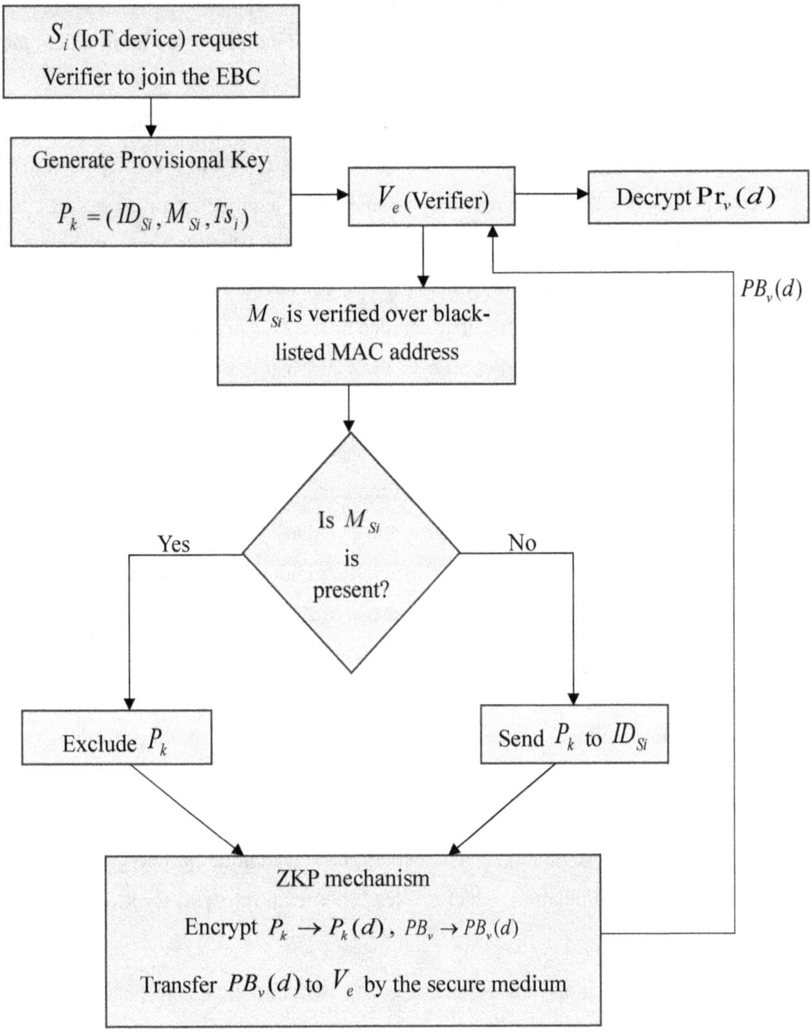

Fig. 3.2 Registration and Verification Phase

(c) ZKP Mechanism: The identified nodes are verified using the ZKP. These cryptographic methods allow an individual to show another individual whether or not the assertion has accurate without disclosing the actual facts. ZKP is utilized in the Ethereum ledger to enable safe data authentication without disclosing private information, preserving confidentiality and confidentiality. This is particularly helpful in settings where confidentiality of information is crucial, such as IoT-based medical facilities. Through incorporating ZKP, Ethereum may confirm the legitimacy of transaction or data modifications on its ledger without having to reveal the data's true information, protecting individual security, and adhering to protection laws.

Through offering limited access without sacrificing the confidentiality of data, ZKP offers an extra layer of protection. ZKP protocols can confirm that the person making the demand has the required credential whenever an equipment or user seeks access to confidential information without disclosing the data itself. In IoT-based medical services, where several devices and individuals utilize confidential information, this capability is crucial. Each communication will be handled by the ZKP in a way that keeps the framework from allowing unknown individuals to view or change private information without the proper authorization. In addition, because the proof does not provide any information than could be detected or abused, ZKP guards against MITM cyberattacks. Every validated transaction has permanently logged on Ethereum's distributed record, thus any attempt at modifying information will become instantly visible.

Because guaranteeing only officially validated, confidentiality operations are documented on a distributed ledger, the usage of ZKP enhances this protection even more. Because of Ethereum's decentralized architecture and the fact that every access occurrence is validated by ZKP, this combination guarantees that information is not only impenetrable but also makes illegal changes exceedingly challenging. With confirming operations without disclosing private information, ZKP on the Ethereum platform offers a strong mechanism for maintaining the confidentiality of data while guaranteeing adherence to stringent privacy regulations. This encryption technique protects against unwanted accessing and manipulation, which makes it particularly useful for safe IoT and medical solutions.

The ZKP aims to authenticate S_i without exposing personal information. Establisher and analyzer-based demanding techniques are taken into consideration within the ZKP. The EBC, S_i is the establisher and V_e is the analyzer. V_e indicates certain questions for the establisher and examines the response to determine the correctness of the establisher.

(d) Encryption and Decryption: After the verification of V_e, the private and the public keys are generated. The Elliptic Curve Cryptography (ECC) is used encoding procedure.

The secret key SK_{Si} for the encryption is evaluated based on to add the PB_{Si} (public key of ith the sensor), PR_{Si} (the private key of ith the sensor) and the P_M (prime number). It is expressed as:

$$SK_{Si} = \sum PR_{Si}, PB_{Si}, P_M \tag{3.1}$$

After the successful generation SK_{Si}, the data S_i is encoded. This encoded data is divided into two cipher-texts $(C1, C2)$, and it is given as:

$$C1 = (P_M 1 * P_M) + SK_{Si} \tag{3.2}$$

$$C2 = Mg_{Si} + (P_M 1 * PB_{Si}) + SK_{Si} \tag{3.3}$$

where $P_M 1$ and Mg_{Si} are the first prime number and message obtained by the S_i. At last, the data is decoded by:

$$Mg_{Si} = ((C2 - PB_{Si}) * C1) - SK_{Si} \tag{3.4}$$

(e) Generation of Block and Validation:

Type of Blockchain Deployed: This study deploys a permissioned Ethereum-based blockchain to support secure, auditable, and privacy-preserving operations within IoT-HCS. A permissioned blockchain is selected because healthcare environments involve known and authorized stakeholders (e.g., hospitals, gateways, healthcare providers), and unrestricted public participation is neither required nor desirable due to privacy and compliance constraints. The Ethereum platform is chosen due to the following reasons:

- Smart Contract Support: Enables automated execution of authentication, access control, and data integrity verification.
- Compatibility with ZKP: Supports privacy-preserving verification mechanisms essential for sensitive healthcare data.
- Mature Tooling and Ecosystem: Facilitates reproducibility through well-documented APIs, development frameworks, and testing tools.
- Fine-Grained Access Control: Permissioned deployment allows controlled participation of network entities while retaining decentralization benefits.

The blockchain network consists of authorized validator nodes operated by trusted healthcare infrastructure components such as hospital servers and edge gateways.

Consensus Algorithm Deployed: The proposed framework employs a PoA consensus algorithm for block generation and validation.

Rationale for Selecting PoA: PoA is selected over alternatives such as PoW and PoS due to the following considerations:

- Low Computational Overhead: PoA eliminates resource-intensive mining operations, making it suitable for IoT-HCS environments.
- Low Latency: Enables faster block confirmation times, which is critical for real-time healthcare data processing.
- Energy Efficiency: Unlike PoW, PoA does not require excessive energy consumption.
- Deterministic Finality: Blocks are finalized quickly without probabilistic forks, ensuring data consistency.
- Controlled Validator Set: Aligns with healthcare trust models, where validator identities are known and managed.

Validator nodes are pre-authorized and periodically audited to maintain trust and system integrity. Validated transactions are grouped into blocks and added to the blockchain through Ethereum's consensus mechanism. Once the registration S_i is completed, the method of building blocks and verification is completed. The procedures used for communication them S_i and V_e are given below:

- Initially, the keys for the S_i like PB_{Si} and PR_{Si} are generated, and the method E_d is used.
- The E_d generates the signature $E_{d\,sig}$ and sends it for verification the S_i.
- The S_i analysis $E_{d\,sig}$ for subsequent communication procedure and when the $E_{d\,sig}$ is matched then S_i requests the $E_{d\,sig}$ to join the EBC.
- The accessible secret is verified by means of the $E_{d\,peer}$ (edge peer nodes), and to confirm if the digital signature was effective or not, a confirmation is transmitted.
- Whether acknowledged is effective, ID_{sdi}^{B} (a new block) is produced and forwarded to the EBC. Finally, the initial information is stored on IPFS. The block preparation and verification procedure are shown in Figure 3.3.

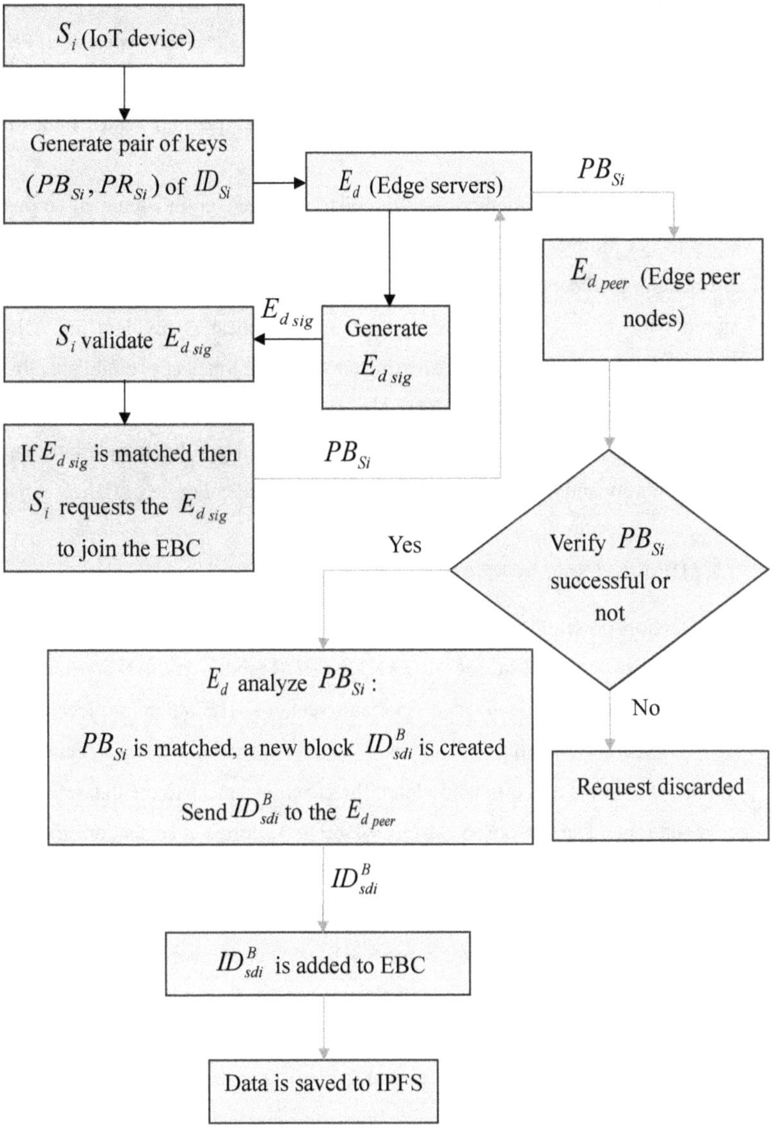

Fig. 3.3 Block Creation and Verification

There are several obstacles to overcome when combining IPFS and Ethereum in IoT-related medical facilities, including slowness in obtaining data, problems with accessibility of data, and the requirement for encrypted access security. Organizations that need immediate data accessibility could become impacted by the variable data retrieving times caused by IPFS's distributed storage. Furthermore, absent active information pins, it may be difficult to retain constant access to vital medical data because IPFS cannot by default ensure accessibility to data. Furthermore, IPFS requires extra layers to protect confidential information from unwanted access because it provides built-in restricting access methods.

The suggested method uses the distributed ledger Ethereum in conjunction with IPFS to get around these issues: Although Blockchain maintains encrypted hashes and ensures the confidentiality of data through recognizing any alteration, IPFS handles huge stored data. only authorized equipment and healthcare providers are able to obtain confidential information thanks to stringent restriction on access established by intelligent contracts on the distributed ledger. This integration strikes a balance between cost-effectiveness, flexibility, and protection, resulting in a solid foundation that meets the confidentiality and reliability needs of IoT-driven medical organizations.

3.2.4 DL-based Security Model

This section presents the effectiveness of DL-based feature extraction mechanism and classify the cyber-attacks using At-GAN-Bi-LSTM model. At-GAN provides the input data to develop the discriminator and generator sections. The attention mechanism of At-Bi-LSTM model retrieves time-stamp feature to improve attack detection accuracy. During the training the model and efficiently learn the attack instances to the dataset and classify the cyber-attacks. The proposed At-GAN-BiLSTM intrusion detection model integrates generative, sequential, and attention-based learning to enhance detection accuracy in IoT-HCS. Initially, a GAN is employed to address class imbalance by synthesizing minority attack samples using a generator composed of fully connected layers (128 and 256 neurons with Rectified Linear Unit (ReLU) activation) and a discriminator with dense layers (256 and 128 neurons using Leaky ReLU, $\alpha = 0.2$). The balanced dataset is then segmented into temporal sequences of 10-time steps and fed into a two-layer Bidirectional LSTM network with 128 hidden units per layer, enabling the model to capture bidirectional temporal dependencies in network traffic flows. An attention mechanism is applied to weight the most discriminative temporal features, followed by a fully connected Softmax layer for binary or multi-class classification. The model is trained using the Adam optimizer with a learning rate of 0.001, batch size of 64, dropout rate of 0.3, and 100 training epochs, ensuring stable convergence, reduced false alarm rates, and robust intrusion detection performance.

An excellent method to evaluate the effectiveness of DL-based feature retrieval and classifying are to use the At-GAN-Bi-LSTM to identify cyberattacks. At-GAN uses the provided input data to develop the discriminator and generator properties. In this case, the attention method retrieves time-related characteristics, and the At-Bi-LSTM is regarded as a feature-extracting framework. Additionally, to improve attack detection accuracy, the At-GAN-BiLSTM model leverages an attention technique that integrates the advantages of GANs and BiLSTM models. For training the model and efficiently add appropriate attack instances to the dataset, the at-GAN module first creates accurate simulated assault strategies. By revealing possible attack situations this adversarial method improves the model's capacity to distinguish between benign and malevolent attempts.

This data is subsequently processed by the BiLSTM layer, which makes it appropriate for network traffic analysis by capturing temporal and sequential trends in neither direction. Through giving more weight to important attributes or stages of time, the attention method helps the privacy model concentrate on important information in intricate traffic movements. This focused strategy improves the efficiency of detection, particularly for risks that are subtle or dynamic. The At-GAN-BiLSTM approach is better flexible and capable to identify novel and complex attack types without requiring a great deal of user involvement than standard IDS techniques, which could rely on preset rules or less complex algorithmic learning techniques. Additional At-GAN-BiLSTM architecture offers a reliable, correct, and flexible approach for real-time intrusions recognition in dynamic situations by fusing GAN-based data enhancement, BiLSTM's sequencing interpreting, and the emphasis available through attention layers. The complete architecture of the proposed Attention-Integrated Generative Adversarial Network with Bidirectional Long Short-Term Memory (AI-GAN-BiLSTM) model, used as a DL-based security module for intrusion detection.VI. Three vital components–GAN, BiLSTM and attention mechanism are incorporated in the framework to learn complex temporal patterns well and enhance anomaly detection performance.

The deep-learning based security model in this study is AI-GAN_BiLSTM, as shown the Figure 3.4. The architecture combines GAN formulated adversarial training, attention-guided weighted feature selection mechanism and BiLSTM based temporal modeling to improve the detection of anomalies in IoT environment.

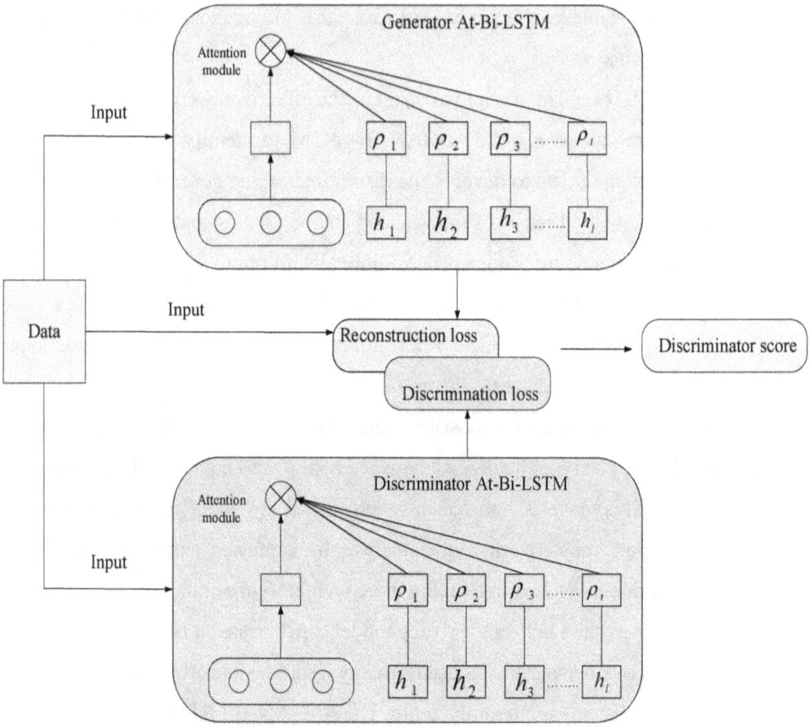

Fig. 3.4 Structure of At-GAN-Bi-LSTM

3.2.4.1 Overall Architecture

The AI-GAN-BiLSTM is comprised of two adversarial modules: a generator (G), and a discriminator (D). Both are instantiated using BiLSTM with attention mechanism, which encourages the learning of consistent temporal representation procedure in the adversarial framework. Model input is pre-processed network traffic features obtained from IoT data streams.

3.2.4.2 Incorporation of Attention Mechanism

The attention mechanism is used in front of the BiLSTM layers on both generator and discriminator as illustrated in Figure 3.4. The attention layer, for a given input feature sequence, calculates importance weights for each time step to enable the model to pay more attentions to traffic segments which are most informative of the malicious behaviors.

Mathematically, given hidden state sequence h_t, attention weights α_t are computed using a scoring function and a subsequent softmax layer. Then the weighted representation will be passed to BiLSTM layers. Such a mechanism allows the model to concentrate on the important temporal patterns, and enhance the detection accuracy for rare and low-frequency attacks. With attention included in both adversarial parts, the model guides what is important and guarantees that discriminating features are uniformly emphasized for both data generation and classification.

3.2.4.3 Generator Network

The generator (G) learns the distribution of malicious traffic and produces synthetic attack examples like the real intrusion patterns. The generator originally leverages an attention mechanism for feature weighting, and is then composed of BiLSTM layers to capture bidirectional temporal correlations in the input data. The samples produced in this manner are fed to the discriminator during training. This adversarial mechanism helps to increase the under-represented attack classes, alleviating class imbalance and enhancing the robustness of IDS model.

3.2.4.4 Discriminator Network

The Discriminator (D) is fed both real network traffic and synthetic samples produced by the Generator. Like generator, it applies attention-based feature weighting followed by BiLSTM layers to learn distinct temporal features. The discrimination outputs the classification probability (i.e., normal/anomalous) of the input sample. By adversarial training, the discriminator can recognize more complicated new attack batches.

3.2.4.5 GAN Loss Functions

The AI-GAN-BiLSTM training is driven by adversary and reconstruction loss, similarly to Figure 3.4.

- Adversarial Loss: The adversarial loss enables the competition between generator and discriminator. The generator tries to play a statistical member against the discriminator, while it simultaneously plays as much as possible a bad feature in favor of the real features. This loss pushes the generator to generate more realistic attack samples.

- Reconstruction Loss: In order to have the generated samples retain actual temporal and statistical properties of real attacks, a reconstruction loss (e.g., mean squared error) is included. This loss encourages the real attack samples and generated samples to be indistinguishable from each other, mitigating GAN training instability and enhancing sample quality.

The optimisation objective is an overall weighted combination of adversarial and reconstruction losses that lead to stable convergence process and enhanced anomaly detection performance.

3.2.4.6 End-to-End Functionality

The generator and discriminator are optimized iteratively during training by adversarial learning. After training, the discriminator is regarded as the resulting IDS model. The attention-BiLSTM layers compute over the coming network traffic, which is used to decide if a transaction was normal or abnormal in an on-line way.

3.2.4.7 Summary

In summary, as seen in Figure 3.4, the system's architecture is strongly coupled:

- Attention mechanisms further contribute to the feature importance in the temporal domain,
- BiLSTM layers learn both left context and right context dependencies.
- Moreover, adversarial learning of GAN is employed to enhance robustness via synthetic data generation, and
- Hybrid loss functions ensure stable training and high detection accuracy.

In the generator-discriminator approach, At-BiLSTM is used to determine which characteristics are eliminated through the forget gate. The updated features were added using that forget gate, which is described as:

$$f_g = Sig\,(U_f[h_{t-1}, y_t] + c_f \tag{3.5}$$

where Sig is the sigmoid function, h_{t-1}, U_f is the model's parameters and y_t are the earlier output and input. Let the input of At-BiLSTM be $Y = \{y_1, y_2, \dots y_m\}$, then the forward and backward LSTMs are given as h_t^f and h_t^b.

$$h_t^b = LSTM^b(y_t, h_{t+1}^b) \tag{3.6}$$

$$h_t^b = LSTM^b(y_t, h_{t+1}^b) \tag{3.7}$$

Equations (6) and (7) obtain the hidden state, and it is given as:

$$H = \{h_1^f, h_t^b\}, \ldots, \{h_n^f, h_n^b\} \tag{3.8}$$

The attention unit is used to ascertain the relationship between the input and concealed layers as well as the significance of the current input; it is provided as:

$$U = \sum_{j=1}^{m} softmax(BiLSTM(Y, H))y_i \tag{3.9}$$

Where, H The generator can maximize the network's parameters if the secret data depends around the At-Bi-LSTM framework. The generator's result serves as the discriminator's input. The generator could enhance the training capabilities of At-GAN throughout learning. Allow the phase of training generator data to be provided.as $G_{At-Bi-LSTM}$. The input parameter is expressed as $\{y_1, y_2, \ldots, y_n\}$, and the respective output of a generator is given as:

$$E(Y) = -\sum_{j=1}^{m} \rho(y_i) \log \rho(y_i) \tag{3.10}$$

First, the residuals' testing interval is provided as below.:

$$S = | Y_{test} - G_{At-Bi-LSTM}(M_k) | \tag{3.11}$$

where M_k is the sequence of the model M, and Y_{test} is the test data.

For getting optimized M_k, M_1 It develops at randomly, and similarities is found using a particular equation 12:

$$Min_{Mk} E(Y_{test}, G_{At-Bi-LSTM}(M_k)) = Similarity(Y_{test}, G_{At-Bi-LSTM}(M_k)) \tag{3.12}$$

The optimization M_k is used to calculate the reconstructed cost and is provided in equation 13:

$$R(y_{test}^t) = \sum_{j=1}^{m} |y_{test,j}^t - G_{At-Bi-LSTM}(M_{k,j}^t)) \tag{3.13}$$

The equation 14 is used to obtained by adding the sum of the discriminating loss and restoration loss:

$$Loss_{test}^t = \alpha R(y_{test}^t) + (1-\alpha) D_{At-Bi-LSTM}(y_{test}^t) \tag{3.14}$$

where α has become the variable used to modify the intrusion identification system.

3.2.5 Pseudo-Code Logic for the Blockchain Enabled IoT Model for Secure Data Transmission

The pseudo-code in Table 3.3 describes a secure IoT data transmission process: first authenticate the IoT devices with ZKP, and then verify their data by means of a DL-based IDS. In the case of legitimate traffic, data is encrypted and stored in IPFS, resulting in the hash of the IPFS being, at this point, a validated transaction in blockchain, which guarantees integrity, privacy, and non-repudiation.

Table 3.3 Pseudo Code for Blockchain Enabled IoT Model for Secure Data Transmission

```
Input: IoT device data, device ID, network parameters
Output: Secure validated block and encrypted data stored in IPFS

Begin
  Initialize Ethereum Blockchain, IPFS, ZKP authentication, IDS
model
  Do While (IoT devices request transmission)
    Generate device keys and signature
    Verify device using ZKP authentication
    Encrypt data and send for IDS verification
    If attack detected, reject request and block device
    else store encrypted data in IPFS and get hash
    Create transaction and validate using consensus
    Add new block and send acknowledgment
  End While
End
```

3.3 Proposed Model 2: Enhancing the LoRaWAN P/S IoT Data Sharing Model using Middleman for Smart Grid Application

- The P/S Protocol used for communication is MQTT, which uses an Agent to transmit the data among P and S on certain Subjects.
- The LoRaWAN module permits an accurate emulation of the LoRa communications' Physical Layers on NS-3. It features LoRa-specific abstractions like Network Servers and Gateways as well as the ability to customise the physical settings.

- We designed and implemented such a system in this study that enables Topic-based information exchange among networks nodes in NS3 by integrating MQTT functionalities into the LoRaWAN module.

3.3.1 Enhanced LoRaWAN-based Secure Data Transmission

The improved LoRaWAN architecture has the goal of addressing the restrictions inherent to typical LoRaWAN deployments, mainly those related to limited security properties, scalability problems, and vulnerability against network-level attacks over large-scale IoT domains. The proposed improvement address security, dependability and data transmission efficiency which can be integrated with blockchain and Artificial Intelligence-based Intrusion Detection Systems (AI-IDSs).

3.3.1.1 Baseline LoRaWAN Architecture

Basic LoRaWAN architecture is composed the following elements:
(i) End devices (IoT nodes),
(ii) LoRa gateways, and
(iii) Network and application servers.

End devices utilize Chirp Spread Spectrum (CSS) modulation for low power, long range communication. The gateways are transparent relays, and they forward packets to the network server which performs device authentication, packet de-duplication, and data routing. Nevertheless, the classic LoRaWAN mainly employs static cryptographic keys and lacks intrusion awareness, which makes it susceptible to various kinds of attacks such as replay attack, impersonation, and packet injection.

3.3.1.2 Proposed Enhancements to LoRaWAN

Below we detail about the improved LoRaWAN framework at network and application layers.

(a) Enhanced Security Mechanisms

To enhance the security, the enhanced LoRaWAN uses:

- Dynamic rather than static keys, reducing the risk of long-term key exposure.
- Reinforced authentication at the network server for checking who sends data.

- Secure payload encapsulation, maintaining data confidentiality and integrity across the network.

These mechanisms mitigate weakness associated with spoofing, replay and unauthorized access.

(b) Improved Data Reliability and Integrity

The improved structure increases the reliability of data by:

- Adaptive Transmission Control (ATC): ATC adapts between transmitting parameters (e.g., spreading factor and data rate) according to the network status.
- Using smart packet checking at the network server to screen out abnormal or malicious packets.

This leads to a lower packet loss and more reliable data delivery even in dense scenarios of the IoT.

(c) Integration with AI-Based Intrusion Detection

Unlike the typical LoRaWAN, the improved way also can directly connect with the AI-GAN-BiLSTM intrusion detection. The network traffic received from the LoRaWAN server is delivered to the DL based security model for real-time investigation. Temporality of the traffic is inspected to find anomalies from various behaviors, such as flooding and timings. With this integration comes a proactive attack detection that is not available in traditional LoRaWAN systems.

(d) Scalability and Energy Efficiency

The improved LoRaWAN preserves the low-power characteristics of the regular LoRaWAN, while enabling large scale. The efficient scheduling and adaptive setting of transmission parameters at client devices reduce the energy consumption and prolong network lifetime, even on the cost of enhanced security processing.

(e) Advantages over Conventional LoRaWAN

The enhanced LoRaWAN framework provides:

- Stronger security and authentication
- Improved data integrity and reliability
- Seamless integration with AI intrusion detection
- Scalability for large IoT deployments

- Design for power scale-down to resource limited devices

Therefore, the proposed enhanced LoRaWAN architecture is much superior to the conventional LoRaWAN in terms of added security features and ATC, including AI-based intrusion detection mechanism, enabling secure data delivery.

3.3.2 MQTT

The MQTT protocol has become the most well-liked and extensively utilized M2M networking protocols. It is an easy-to-use protocol for interconnecting distant components, particularly ones with low bandwidth connectivity. As an intermediary, a broker retains the data and filters it according to the S in question before forwarding it to the legitimate receiver. Instead of a direct connection among the sender and the recipient, transmissions have categories based on categories choices. It is not necessary for both the sender and its recipient become recognized or to begin operating at the same time. An MQTT sender can function as additionally writer and a reader (P/S), as seen in Figure 3.5. An MQTT unit or terminal can S to multiple topics and receive data from individuals because to its dual-channel communication capabilities. Furthermore, it offers a variety of performance of service standards depending on the need. being utilized. Security features like TLS may be added to further protect transmission. This layer of safety can then be used by the agent to confirm the real existence of the user. A connector (sensor network gateway) might be positioned adjacent to the intermediary to build an improved MQTT-SN variation, that supports multicast (or broadcast), as MQTT depends on unicasts compared to multicasting immediately. In this arrangement, the router and broker are both connected via UDP-based multicasts.

Therefore, to enable this functionality in the system, the creators combine the MQTT protocol alongside a LoRaWAN router. According to the subject area, any device using the MQTT framework can P/S to content. A Base Station may function as a web server in an intelligent grid setting to gather massive quantities of information to make the required choices.

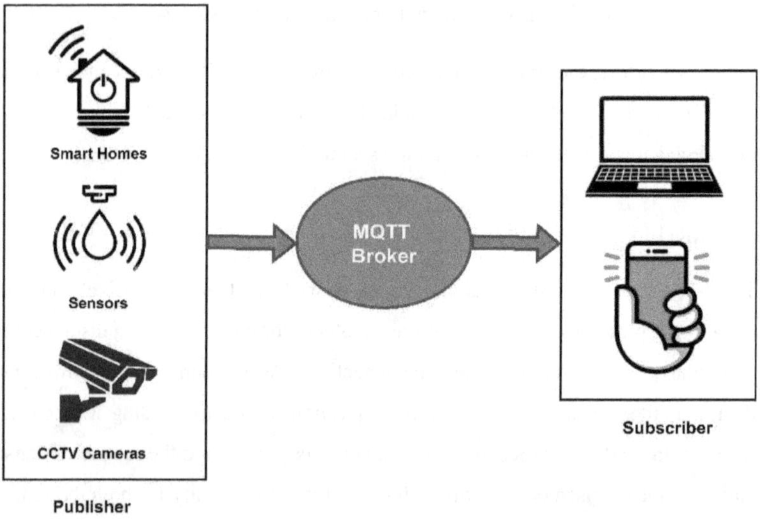

Fig. 3.5 Conceptual Intelligent Grid System based on MQTT

3.3.3 OPC-UA

MQTT over IoT and OPC-UA have comparable because the latter uses the P/S technique to communicate data, while OPC-UA, providing a common system, enables multiple devices to communicate by transferring data via request/response. Furthermore, intelligent grids and operational automation systems commonly employ the P/S framework known as OPC UA. As a result, as shown in Figure 3.6, bidirectional communication occurs among all devices via the Broker. Polling customers at scheduled times is made feasible through not polling the server. This kind of idea is also great for exploiting transmitting abilities for connecting to multiple devices immediately without consuming more data because of unicast communications. Monitoring each networks instrument, data structure, and function is made feasible by employing an OPC-UA platform based on P/S, which enables the invocation of particular functions like copying, editing, and others.

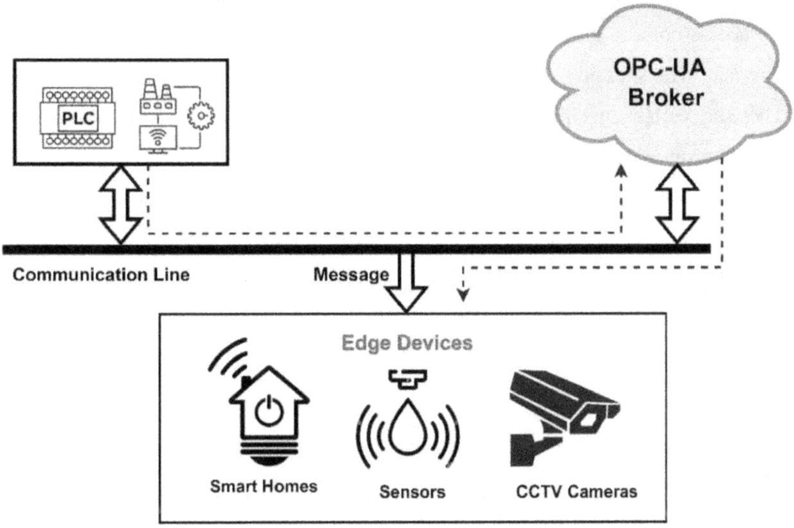

Fig. 3.6 MQTT-based IoT Communication Architecture (Zalte et al. 2020)

3.3.4 IDS

By employing a P/S model and a data-central system, a decentralized interaction broadly known as Data Distributed Systems satisfies the needs of highly adaptable and distributed programs for exchange of data. The IDS's framework is made up of numerous subjects, each of which contains a variety of data items determined by a particular key value. While delivering the data processes, publishers, usually are primarily data repositories, will decide what kind of occurrence will be documented and whether it will be published to specific topics. On the other hand, subscribers will highlight the read kind after obtaining the data processing and declare their preference whenever subscribing within a subject.

3.3.5 LoRa Scheme

The LoRaWAN represents the primary idea and collection of resources the writers use in this investigation. A succinct analysis is given in this paragraph. LoRaWAN provides a reduced data transfer strategy that is well-suited for large regions when nodes are spatially apart from one another, as already stated. LoRaWAN is designed to have a small data rate capability, a long broadcast spectrum, and minimal energy usage. The LoRaWAN system's star-of-stars structure enables information to be transferred between endpoints to a distant location across an IP-based wired connection following initially being collected through the access point in the center. The LoRaWAN architecture consists of four levels: LoRa Physical, Transmission Protocol, Networking Protocol, and Geographical Parameters. These are certain specific factors that vary by location because distinct areas are required to follow varying rates. Three distinct terminal types, designated A, B, and C, are supported by the LoRaWAN specification. A and B nodes are constrained in terms of receiving messages and preserving energy, but C nodes remain unrestricted. Additionally, the switching frequency of nodes A and B are quite minimal. As seen in Figure 3.7, LoRa also offers an internet-based server, like The Things Network, making implementation and connectivity easy.

3.3.6 Environment of LoRaWAN

In the LoRaWAN Module the authors will be employing permits an accurate emulation of the LoRa communications' physical layers on NS-3. It features LoRa-specific abstractions like Network Servers and Gateways as well as the ability to customise the physical settings

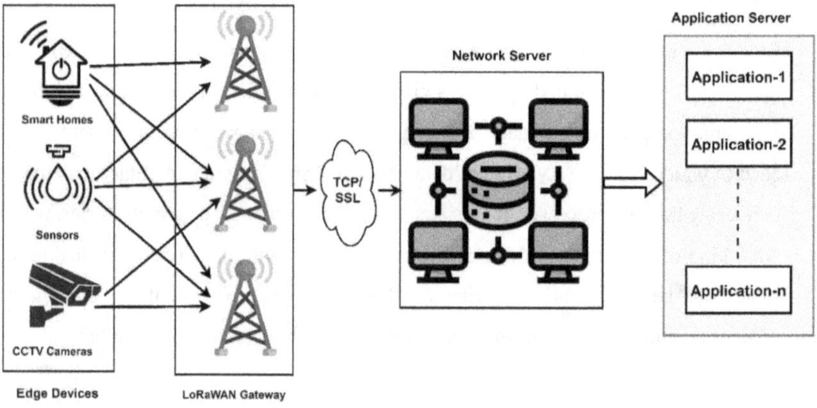

Fig. 3.7 Conceptual Model of LoRaWAN

This indicates why it has become so common in the research that is currently available (Alsaedi et al., 2020). LoRaWAN approach vulnerability to downstream action, low Excellent Spreading Rates, duty periods, or combination is a major disadvantage, though, as it would adversely affect uplink and downlink efficiency (Unal et al. 2021,

Kumari et al. 2023). As stated by Alkadi et al. (2020), LoRaWAN has a maximum possible transmission rate of 27 kbps if utilized with SF=7 and BW=500 kHz, which limits its data rate. The data rate restriction, still allows it to be appropriate for a wide range of IoT scenarios in which devices produce and exchange data with one another. The use of P/S systems is becoming increasingly popular in a variety of fields, such as production, transport, the electricity grid, etc, without the help of maintaining oversight server that gathers information and utilizes the possibilities. MQTT has become the most widely utilised protocols across a variety of IoT nodes as well as regulations when it comes to the employment of a broker among the P/S.

Since NS-3 supports several communication standards, MQTT is unsuitable for widespread IoT solutions with NS-3 since it is frequently utilized with popular protocols including Wi-Fi and LTE networks. Therefore, it is necessary to combine the widely employed LoRaWAN Unit alongside the P/S structure of NS-3. Additionally, it will facilitate the development of NS-3 scaling evaluations. It should be noted that a broker within an MQTT system and the Network Server abstraction in LoRaWAN operate quite identically provides additional support regarding their interaction. For the reasons described above, the main goal of this study is to shed light on LoRaWAN's performance using employed WAN standard MQTT.

3.3.7 MQTT Tag for Two-way Communication

A TAG is specified as a virtual class within NS-3. As shown in Figure 3.8, clients that would like to utilize a customized tag must supply a ́distinctive class specification. GetSerializedSize(), Serialize(), and Deserialize() are among the procedures that NS3 automatically calls when using the AddPacketTag() and RemovePacketTag() interfaces. A great deal of attention must be taken to guarantee that this strategy is applied appropriately because any modification to their specification might result in problems after assembly.
In order to use the P/S structure, we need to specify the kinds of control messages which the broker is willing to receive. The message category which will be delivered included within the message tag themselves. Given this approach, writers only explain the P/S message categories.

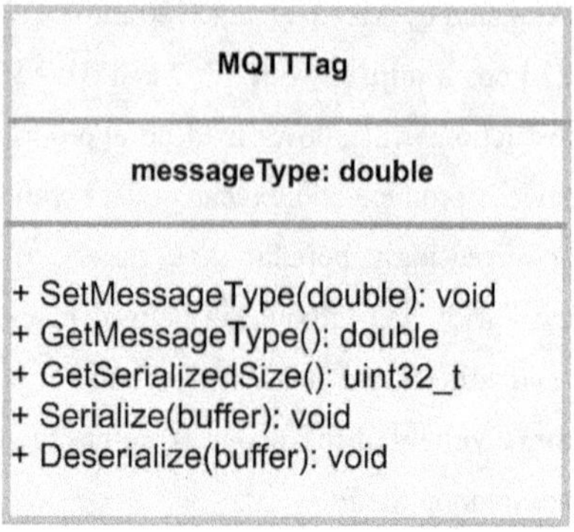

Fig. 3.8 UML Structure of P/S Tag

Further techniques must be implemented within the TAG type just to obtain accessibility to the information which has been collected via the previously specified strategies. Assuming the hard-coded parameters are the only ones meant for the Customized Tag, then no further adjustments are required. Since clients become able to specify the type of text that appears in the tag, the writers will need to put up the sets and receivers associated with the tag. The researchers created the SetType() and GetType() techniques to accomplish this. In order for the broker to deserialize and recover the data after getting it, the techniques will alter the controlling message classes to enable sequential publishing of the data into a frame.

3.3.8 Integration of LORAWAN Architecture

To support this integration, the LoRaWAN–MQTT publish/subscribe model was implemented in the NS-3 simulation platform by adding C++-based extensions to the LoRaWAN Network Server module. The network server was expanded into an MQTT broker, capable of topic-based routing logic based on a std::map container object that maps topics to subscriber node IP addresses. End devices on LoRa either published or subscribed, and gateways flooded packets up to the modified network server. The simulation considered star-of-stars LoRaWAN topology, with controllable parameters such as spreading factor (SF7–SF12), bandwidth (125–500 kHz), transmission power (14 dBm), and duty cycle limited to the typical IoT communication conditions. We then designed custom packet tags to wrap up MQTT control messages so the functions subscribeToTopic(), publishToTopic(), and send() could distribute messages. This architecture enabled the incorporation of MQTT messaging within the LoRaWAN framework together with realistic network behavior as well as facilitated scalable topic-based data distribution for smart grid IoT services.

Several factors, in no specific sequence, led the authors to choose this data form:

- **Special Keys:** It allows just single subject having an identical label to be present since no two parameters can have an identical value.
- **Allocation-aware:** uses an allocation class to flexibly adjust the storage needed and permits a finite number of Topics and locations associated with them.
- **Complexity of Time:** Retrieval frequency rises with $log_{10}(N)$. It might, still vary from $log_2(N)$. Additionally, inserts also match $log_2(N)$.

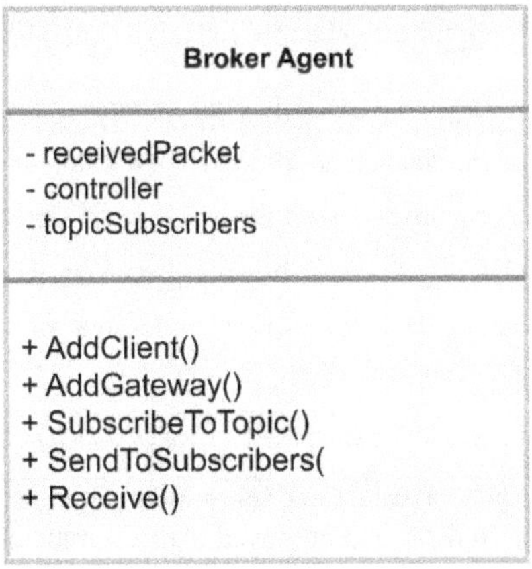

Fig. 3.9 Functional Structure for an MQTT Broker Agent (UML)

The parameters in our map layout will be a listing of the IP addresses of the computers which have this subject associated with every key among the subjects. The logic required to determine what kind of content and route packages from the proper place can then be added to the Network Server's information structure. We are going to refer to the internet connection, which is shown in Figure 3.9, as a Broker. To use this logic, three additional techniques need to be established. The first technique is called SubscribeToTopic(). This process is triggered if the message which the Broker got represented a Subscribe control message. The receiving packet is examined to retrieve the packet's content and the transmitting node's location. The approach then receives the location and subject. Although the link is inserted to the location list related to the subject, the subject line is added as a single of the parameters to the std: map framework.

PublishToTopic(): we implement PublishToTopic(). This process is triggered whenever the broker gets a publishing control message. The authors extracted the topic and the content of the message from the incoming packet. The topic and content are subsequently passed as arguments when the technique is called. The presence of a subject then gets verified. Someone may set up a message to be delivered to the topic subscribers whenever a topic is accessible. To accomplish this, send () has been specified as a further technique. In order to support the NetDevice connected to the Broker, it repeatedly runs and makes another call to transmit (). This technique will be used to get a server that is setup for various NetDevices in order to get the alien broker.

3.3.9 Pseudo-Code Logic for the enhanced LoRaWAN MQTT P/S using Middleman

The pseudo-code in Table 3.4 describes an enhanced LoRaWAN-based MQTT P/S messaging through a middleman to process forwarding and scheduling of published messages. The mediator helps to lessen the overload on the broker and speed up message delivery, improves reliability by using organized transfer queues, and allows for efficient communication by sending data to subscribed nodes in a way that uses resources wisely.

Table 3. 4 Pseudo Code for Enhanced LoRaWAN MQTT P/S using Middleman

Input: Sensor publish data, topic subscription requests
Output: Reduced delay and improved PDR via middleman forwarding

```
Begin
   Initialize LoRaWAN gateway, MQTT broker, and Middleman node
   Do While (Network is active)
      Receive publish/subscription request from IoT nodes
      If request is SUBSCRIBE, update topic table
      If request is PUBLISH, forward to Middleman
      Middleman queues, schedules, and relays data to broker
      Broker delivers data to all subscribed nodes
      Update PDR and delay statistics
   End While
End
```

3.4 Discussion: Blockchain-based IoT Model vs Enhanced LoRaWAN-based Model Comparison

Two solutions to the issues faced by communication of IoT data are blockchain-driven secure IoT data transmission and an improved LoRaWAN message channelling architecture. While they have similar goal in mind, i.e., to facilitate the sharing of IoT data, their goals as well as architecture and performance vary remarkably.

The proposed blockchain-based IoT model focuses primarily on providing security, trustworthiness, and Date integrity in the context of IoT. Drawing from the decentralized ledger and smart contract writing capability of blockchains, it guarantees dates tamper resistance for data storage, secure authentication, and transparent access control. It can effectively address problems like data tampering, unauthorized access and single-point failure encountered in centralized IoT. Nevertheless, the use of blockchain contributes extra overhead in terms of computation and communication that might cause added latency and energy consumption as for resource constrained IoT devices.

The improved LoRaWAN method, conversely, is aimed at optimizing the efficient low-power and scalable data transmission in massive IoT applications. LoRaWAN's long-distance, low-power communication capabilities are optimal for applications including smart grid, environmental monitoring and industrial IoT. The improved model enhances the data dissemination by employing optimized P/S mechanisms, which results in decreased energy consumption and increased scalability. However, despite the basic security features of LoRaWAN, it does not offer sophisticated decentralized trust management and underlying data integrity for several reasons leaving the network susceptible to strong attacks.

In general, blockchain-based IoT model is more appropriate for security-intensive applications where 'trust', and 'privacy' are the main concerns issue of data integrity, such as health care base IoT system and financial based IoT. Conversely, the improved LoRaWAN-based solution is more suitable for such large-scaled low-power IoT networks, and places more emphasis on energy efficiency of devices, coverage, and scalability other than complex security methods. The two approaches are, therefore, synergistic in nature that does not conflict and target different challenges faced during IoT data.

A performance, security, and application suitability comparison between the blockchain-IoT mode and an optimized LoRaWAN approach is presented in Table 3.5.

Table 3.5 Blockchain-based IoT Model vs Enhanced LoRaWAN-based Model Comparison

Feature	**Blockchain-based IoT Model**	**Enhanced LoRaWAN-based Model**
Objective	Secure and trusted data exchange	Energy-efficient, scalable communication infrastructure
Architecture	Decentralized, blockchain-based	LPWAN-centric centralized gateway model
Security level	High (immutability, smart contracts)	Moderate (encryption, basic authentication)
Data integrity	Strong (tamper-proof ledger)	Limited
Latency	Higher due to blockchain operations	Low
Energy efficiency	Moderate to low	High
Scalability	Moderate	High
Application domain	Healthcare industry, finance, sensitive IoT systems	Smart grid, smart city, environmental monitoring

CHAPTER 4

Result Analysis

4.1 Overview

This chapter presents the result analysis of the proposed models and measures the performance using the several evaluation parameters. This chapter also compares the proposed models' results with the existing state-of-the-art or existing methods. The chapter aims to highlight the strengths and weaknesses of each approach in terms of accuracy score, precision rate, recall, F1-score, average delay of node, PDR, and average publish delay (Muneer et al. 2024). By systematically analyzing and contrasting the performance metrics of proposed models, researchers can identify the most effective techniques for securing the data transmission based on blockchain over the IoT environment and the LoRaWAN model based on the P/S mechanism. The model reduces network congestion, improves PDR, and optimizes message transmission delay, making it ideal for smart grid and industrial automation applications.

4.2 Proposed Model 1: Blockchain-Enabled IoT based Model for Secure Data Transmission

All experiments for Model-1 were executed using Python-based implementation on a desktop-class machine with an Intel Core i3 CPU and 8GB RAM, which represents the edge gateway/hospital server/blockchain validator host responsible for running security services such as smart contract interaction, ZKP verification, IPFS interfacing, and IDS inference, rather than the constrained IoT sensor hardware.

In practical IoT-HCS deployments, end devices typically act as lightweight sensing/transmitting nodes, while the computationally intensive operations (block validation, verification, and DL inference) are offloaded to the gateway/edge tier. Hence, the reported hardware configuration reflects the compute tier used for orchestration and analysis, while IoT nodes are represented by dataset-driven traffic samples and gateway-mediated security workflow.

Table 4.1 Hyperparameters

Parameters	**Values**
Security Validation	Zero Knowledge Proof
Cryptographic Hash Function	SHA256
Block size	128 Bytes
Optimizer	Adam
Activation function	Softmax
Loss Function	Binary cross-entropy
Batch size	64
Epochs	100
Training: Testing ratio	80:20

Table 4.1 shows the hyperparameters were selected through empirical experimentation, guided by prior studies on DL-based intrusion detection and the computational constraints of IoT-oriented environments (Yu et al. 2023, Neelakandan et al. (2022). The Adam optimizer with a learning rate of 0.001 was adopted to ensure stable and fast convergence without oscillatory behavior. A batch size of 64 was chosen to balance gradient stability and memory efficiency, while 50 training epochs were sufficient to achieve convergence across all datasets without overfitting. The BiLSTM hidden unit size was fixed at 128 to effectively capture temporal dependencies in network traffic while maintaining moderate model complexity. A dropout rate of 0.3 was employed to mitigate overfitting without suppressing critical sequential features. The input sequence length was set to 10 time steps, which provided adequate temporal context for anomaly detection with minimal computational overhead. Additionally, the GAN noise vector dimension of 100 ensured sufficient diversity in synthetic attack samples while preserving training stability.

4.2.1 Performance Evaluation Metrics

In this section the mathematical formulations of the performance evaluation metrics used in this study are defined. These metrics are derived from the confusion matrix, consisting of True Positives (TP), True Negatives (TN), False Positives (FP), and False Negatives (FN) (Muneer et al. 2024).

$$Accuracy = \frac{TP+TN}{TP+TN+FP+FN} \quad (4.1)$$

$$Precision\ (P) = \frac{TP}{TP+FP} \tag{4.2}$$

$$Recall\ (R) = \frac{TP}{TP+FN} \tag{4.3}$$

$$F1 - score = 2 * \frac{P+R}{P+R} \tag{4.4}$$

$$FAR = \frac{FP}{FP+TN} \tag{4.5}$$

$$PDR = \frac{N_{received}}{N_{sent}} \tag{4.6}$$

$$Latancy = \frac{1}{N} \sum_{i=1}^{N} \left(t_{recv}^{(i)} - t_{send}^{(i)} \right) \tag{4.7}$$

4.2.2 Result Analysis on D1

In this section, the effectiveness of the DL-based security framework and the EBC-based security strategy for the D1 is evaluated.

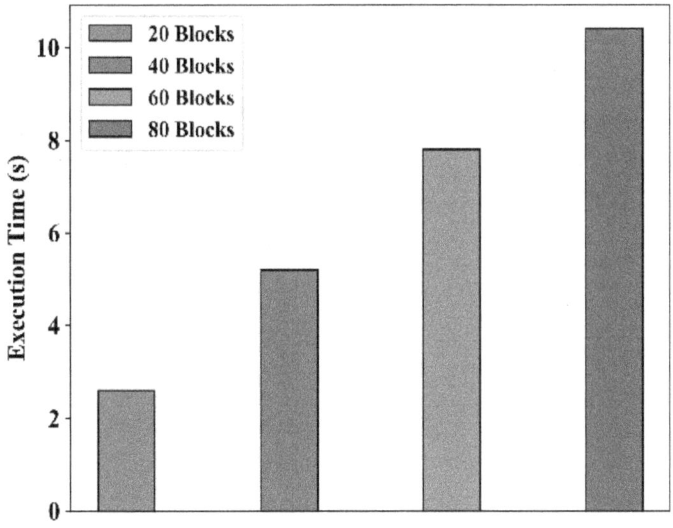

(1)

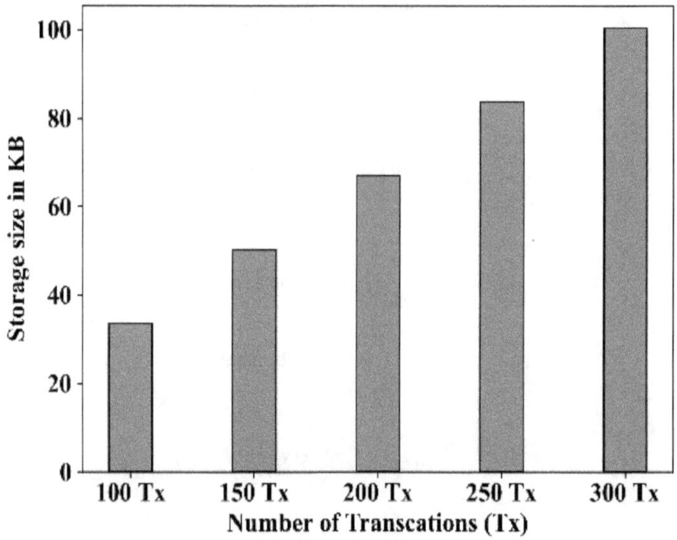
100
80
60
40
20
0
Storage size in KB
100 Tx
150 Tx
200 Tx
250 Tx
300 Tx
Number of Transcations (Tx)

(2)

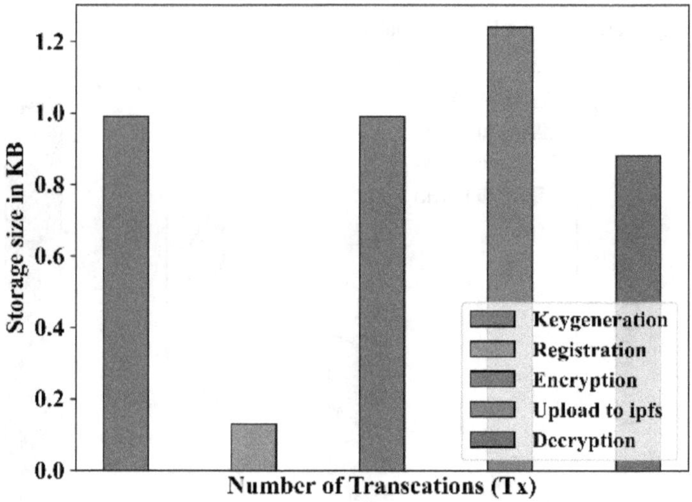
1.2
1.0
0.8
0.6
0.4
0.2
0.0
Storage size in KB
Keygeneration
Registration
Encryption
Upload to ipfs
Decryption
Number of Transcations (Tx)

(3)

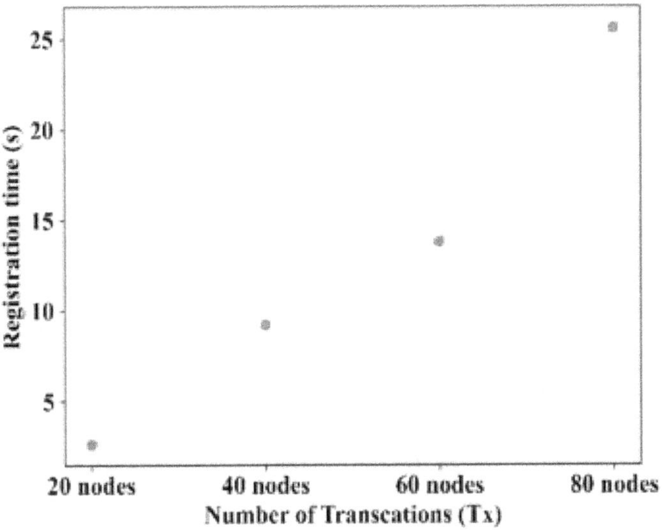

(4)

Fig. 4.1 Performance Analysis of the EBC

The EBC model performance assessment is displayed in Figure 4.1. Several parts are used to validate the produced EBC. When altering the number of blocks, Figure 4.1(1) displays the overall time required for the EBC system to run. It is evident that the processing time increases in tandem with the number of blocks. The capacity to execute transactions in parallel, yet, helps offset the execution time rises, indicating that the framework remains capable of effectively handling larger blockchains. As a result, the Blockchain's operational time is reduced while the number of blocks increases. Figure 4.1 (2) displays several transaction storing sizes. Storage space is required for every transaction on a distributed ledger. This demonstrates how crucial scalable storage options are to managing expanding data in blockchain-driven networks. Sender, recipient, quantity, timestamp, and authentication are among the details included in this data. Additional information results from more transactions, which calls for more storage. The amount of storage needed for key generation, authentication, encoding, IPFS sharing, and decryption is indicated in Figure 4.1 (3). Finally, Figure 4.1 (4) displays the signing-up time when the number of IoT devices is changed from 20 to 80. Increased volume of transactions may result in network overload, which may affect the handling of new entries and lengthen the authorization period.

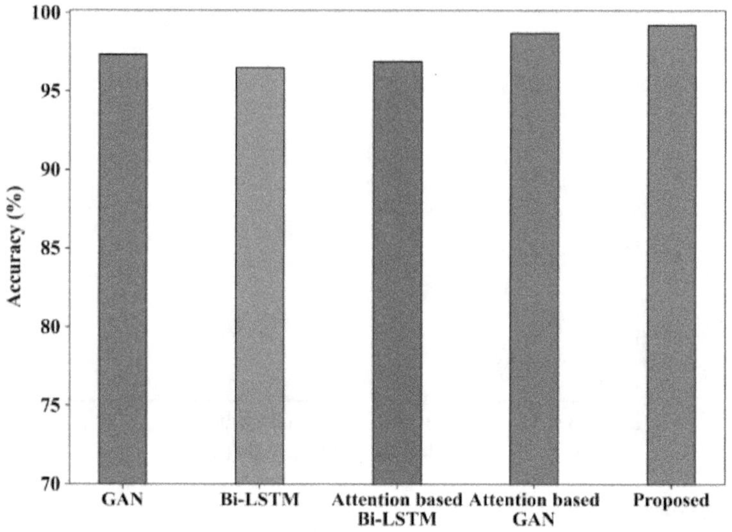

(1)

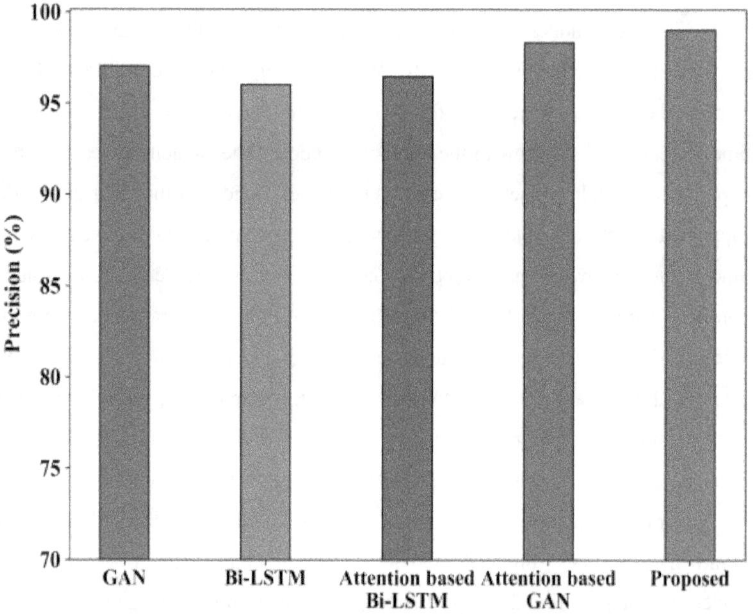

(2)

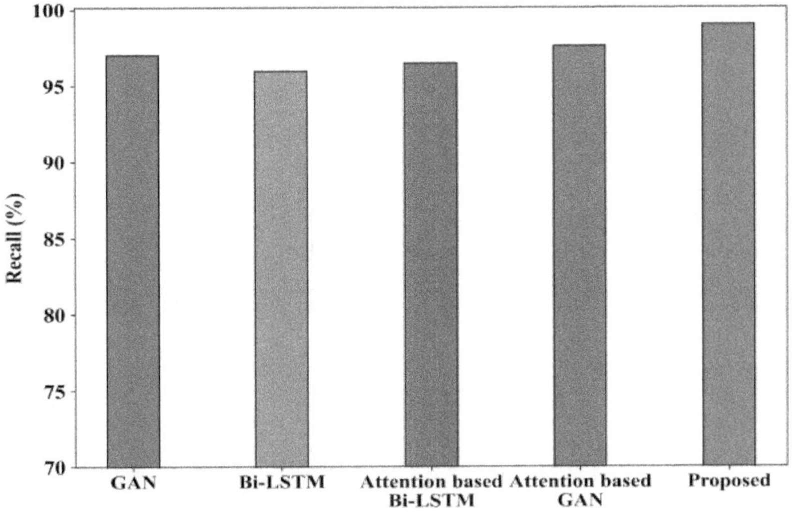
100
95
90
85
80
75
70
Recall (%)
GAN
Bi-LSTM
Attention based Bi-LSTM
Attention based GAN
Proposed

(3)

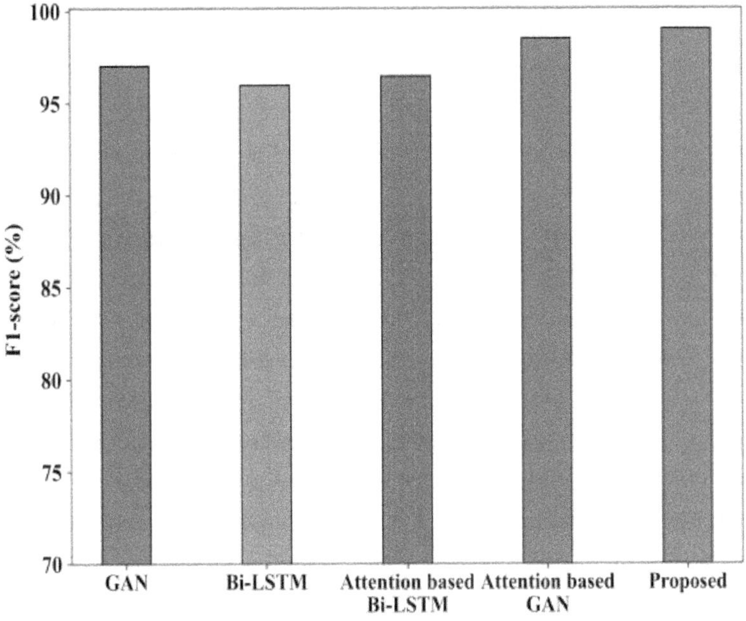
100
95
90
85
80
75
70
F1-score (%)
GAN
Bi-LSTM
Attention based Bi-LSTM
Attention based GAN
Proposed

(4)

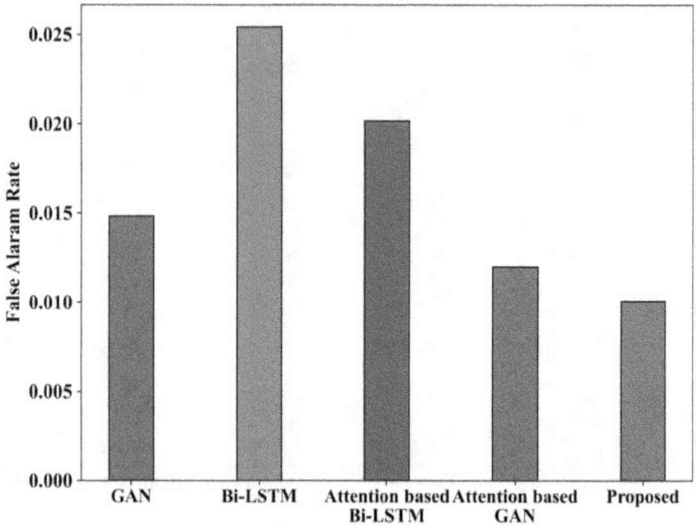

(5)

Fig. 4.2 Evaluation of the Suggested and Traditional DL Architectures' Performances

The ablation investigation of the suggested GAN, Bi-LSTM, and attention-based Bi-LSTM models, along with attention-based GAN and the suggested At-GAN-Bi-LSTM method, is shown in Figure 4.2. Figure 4.2 (1) illustrates how accurate each method is. The suggested At-GAN-Bi-LSTM outperforms techniques such as GAN, Bi-LSTM, and attention-based Bi-LSTM by 99.9%, 2.02%, 2.72%, and 2.41%, respectively. The precision and recall values achieved through the suggested At-GAN-Bi-LSTM are 99.95% and 99.85%, respectively, as shown in Figures 4.2 (2) and 4.2 (3). In a comparable manner, the suggested At-GAN-Bi-LSTM achieves an F1-score value of 99.69% in Figure 4.2 (4), which is 3.12%, 4.25%, and 4.41% higher compared to methods such as GAN, Bi-LSTM, and attention-based Bi-LSTM. A superior attack identification model requires a very low FAR value, as shown in Figure 4.2 (5). The graph shows the actual FAR value for the suggested At-GAN-Bi-LSTM is significantly lower (0.01). The inability to handle sequential relationships, the inability to capture fine-grained abnormalities, and the imperfect unification of attention techniques with extracting features are some of the drawbacks of current methods, such as GAN, Bi-LSTM, Attention-based Bi-LSTM, and Attention-based GAN. These are addressed using the suggested At-GAN-Bi-LSTM, which combines attention processes with GAN and Bi-LSTM. This makes it possible to recognize vulnerabilities in IoT systems more accurately and reliably by improving feature extracting, identification of anomalies, and effectiveness.

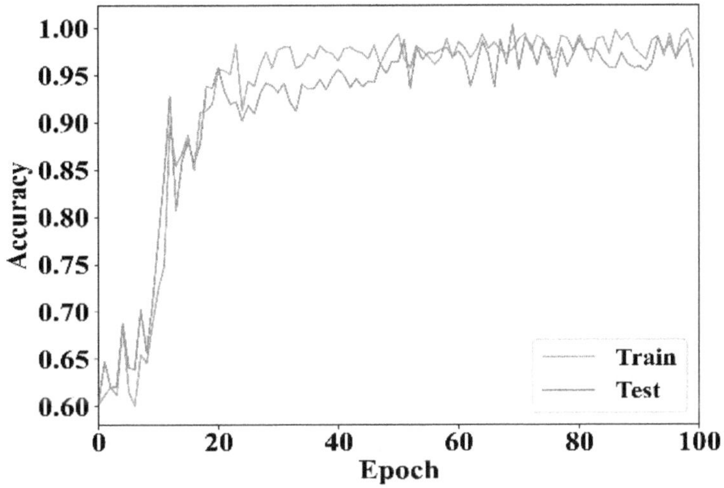

(1)

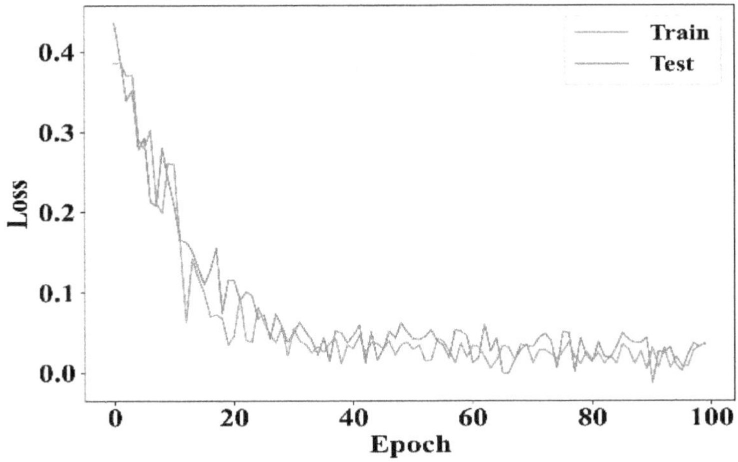

(2)

Fig. 4.3 Training and Testing Analysis of (1) Accuracy and (2) Loss Curves

The accuracy and loss curve evaluation of the suggested At-GAN-Bi-LSTM is shown in Figure 4.3. Figure 4.3 (1) shows that increases in epoch value led to improvements in training and testing performance. The model improves its comprehension of the connections across input characteristics and output labels with every epoch. When evaluating the data, it results in more precise identification. In a comparable manner in Figure 4.3 (2), the loss of testing and training reduces while the epoch value grows. As the model's predictions get closer to the actual labels, it produces predictions that are more reliable and reduces losses.

The suggested At-GAN-Bi-LSTM system's confusion matrix and ROC curve are presented in Figure 4.4 (Zhang et al. 2021). The ROC evaluation of the several approaches is shown in Figure 4.4 (1). In this case, the attention-based Bi-LSTM is 0.98, the suggested At-GAN-Bi-LSTM is 0.99, the GAN's AUC score is 0.985, and the Bi-LSTM is 0.975. The predictive algorithm is more effective at differentiating between positives and negatives with fewer FP if the curve becomes higher at the beginning. Due to their inability to balance TP and FP values, the current models provide lower values on ROC curves. A statistical evaluation of the categorization methods is used to determine accuracy and is shown in Figure 4.4 (2). The matrix shows that 56,328 instances are categorized as non-attacks and 15,093 instances are identified as assaults.

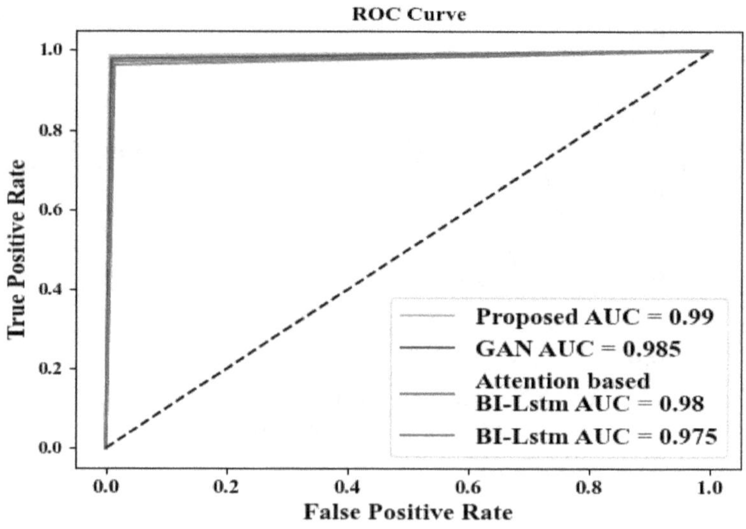

(1)

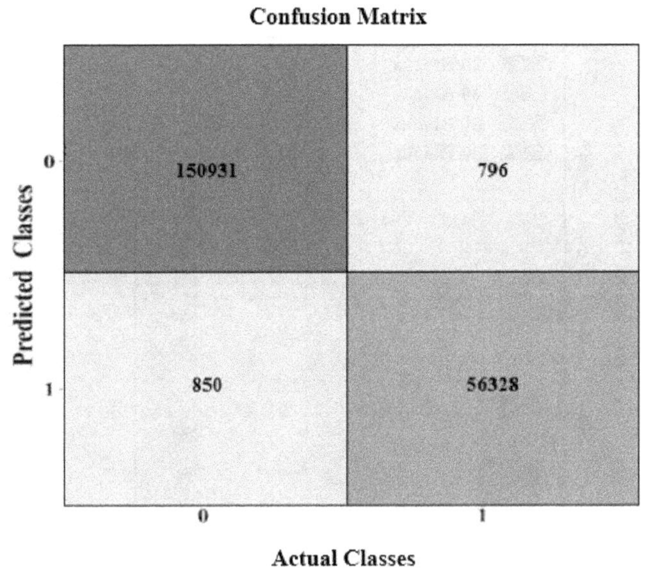

(2)

Fig. 4.4 Effectiveness of (1) ROC Curve and (2) Confusion Matrix of Suggested At-GAN-Bi-LSTM model

The suggested At-GAN-Bi-LSTM system's confusion matrix and ROC curve are presented in Figure 4.4 (Zhang et al. 2021). The ROC evaluation of the several approaches is shown in Figure 4.4 (1). In this case, the attention-based Bi-LSTM is 0.98, the suggested At-GAN-Bi-LSTM is 0.99, the GAN's AUC score is 0.985, and the Bi-LSTM is 0.975. The predictive algorithm is more effective at differentiating between positives and negatives with fewer FP if the curve becomes higher at the beginning. Due to their inability to balance TP and FP values, the current models provide lower values on ROC curves. A statistical evaluation of the categorization methods is used to determine accuracy and is shown in Figure 4.4 (2). The matrix shows that 56,328 instances are categorized as non-attacks and 15,093 instances are identified as assaults.

4.2.3 Result Analysis on D2

In this section, the performance of the DL-based and EBC-based security models for dataset-2 (D2) is covered.

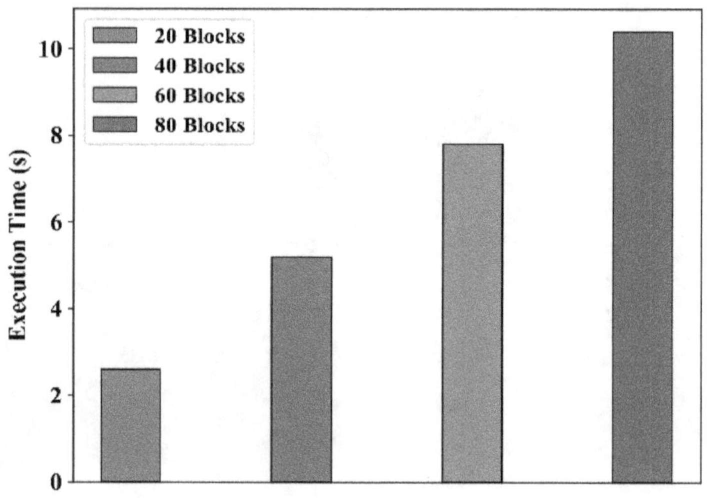
20 Blocks
40 Blocks
60 Blocks
80 Blocks
Execution Time (s)
0
2
4
6
8
10

(1)

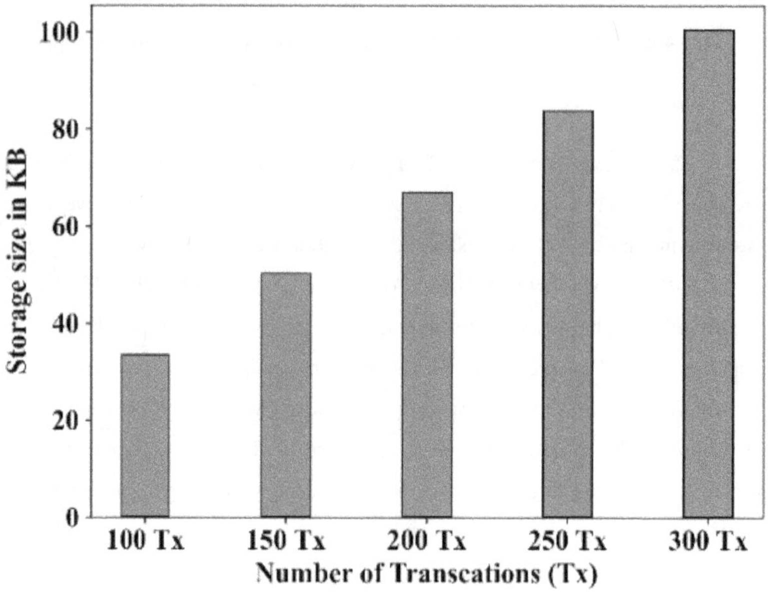
Storage size in KB
0
20
40
60
80
100
100 Tx
150 Tx
200 Tx
250 Tx
300 Tx
Number of Transcations (Tx)

(2)

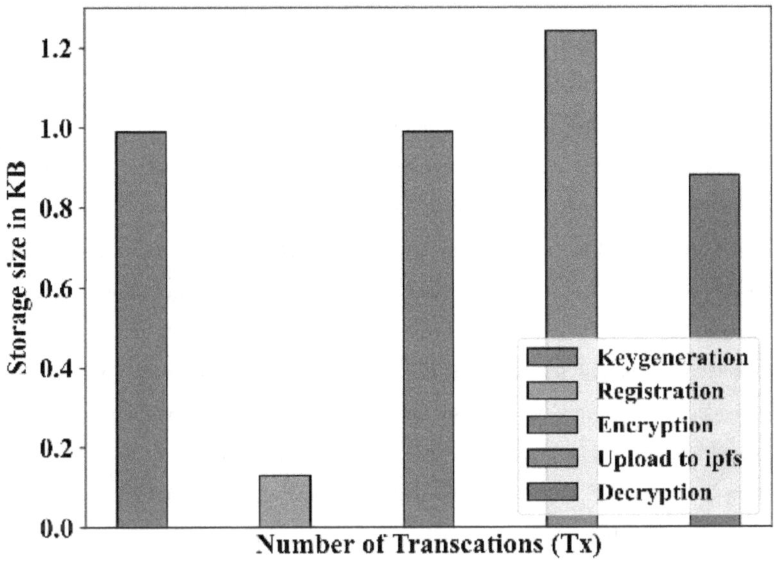

(3)

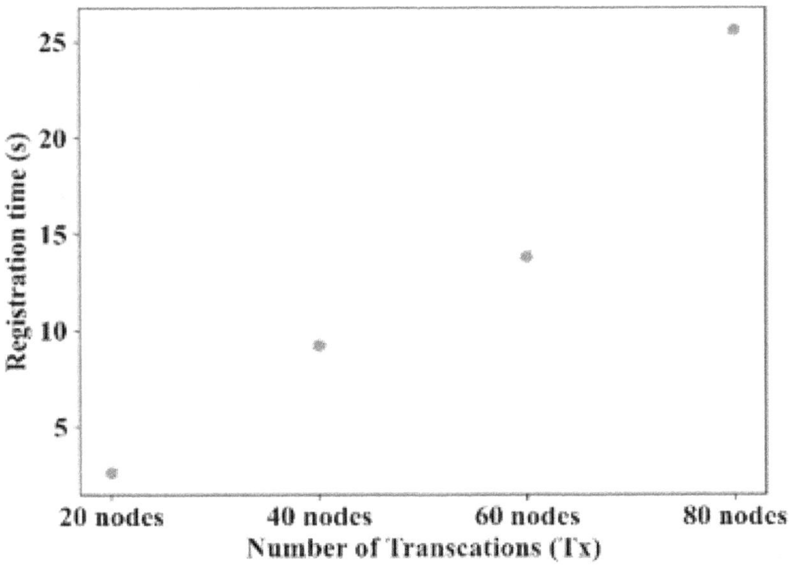

(4)

Fig. 4.5 Evaluation of the EBC's Effectiveness

The effectiveness assessment of the suggested EBC system over D2 is shown in Figure 4.5. The execution time of the Ethereum Blockchain-based security model changes slowly with processed blocks, as shown in Figure 4.5 (1). This overhead is primarily because of the extra computation required for validating transactions and generating blocks. Nevertheless, it is a smooth increasing trend showing the scalability and computation efficiency of the model. The memory consumption is visualized as a function of the number of transactions in Figure 4.5 (2). Memory consumption continues to climb as the blockchain's ledger grows and more transaction metadata is stored. Even with this growth, the memory usage is still in the reasonable level which means that its resource management is efficient. It is evident that the EBC takes only two seconds while considering the twenty blocks. As transactions rise, consequently increases the size of the memories. The data storage amount used for generating keys, enrollment, encrypting it, transferring to IPFS, and decoding is then shown in Figure 4.5 (3). Figure 4.5 (4) illustrates that registration time increases with the number of nodes. According to this data, increasing the number of blocks results in a rise in time taken for execution. The suggested method's overall storage and registration duration grow as the total amount of nodes and operations rises.

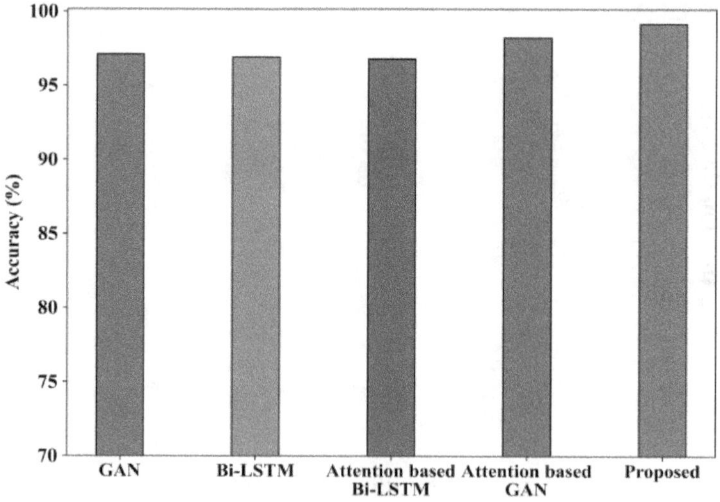

(1)

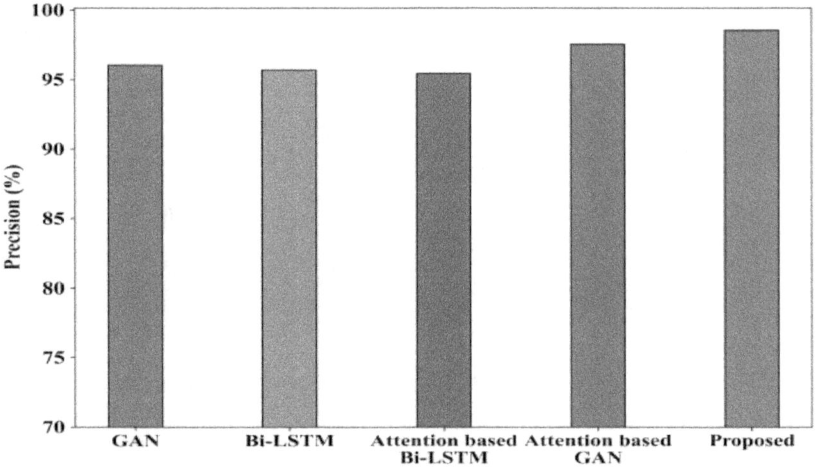
100
95
90
85
80
75
70
Precision (%)
GAN
Bi-LSTM
Attention based Bi-LSTM
Attention based GAN
Proposed

(2)

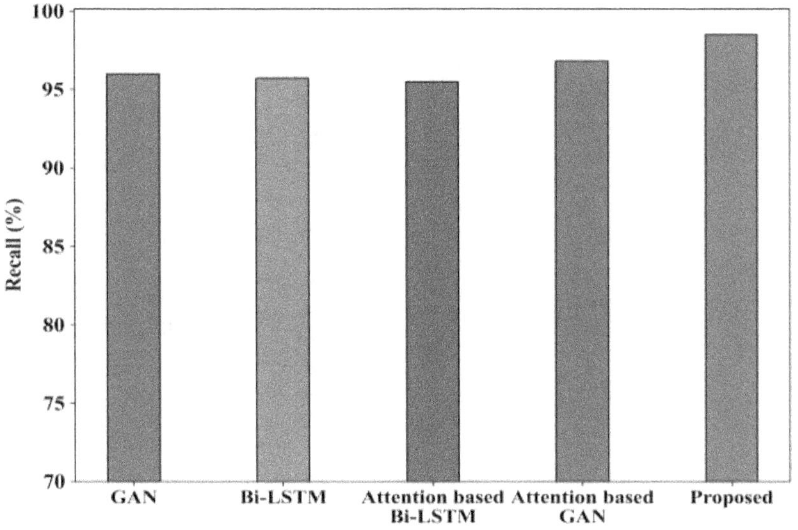
100
95
90
85
80
75
70
Recall (%)
GAN
Bi-LSTM
Attention based Bi-LSTM
Attention based GAN
Proposed

(3)

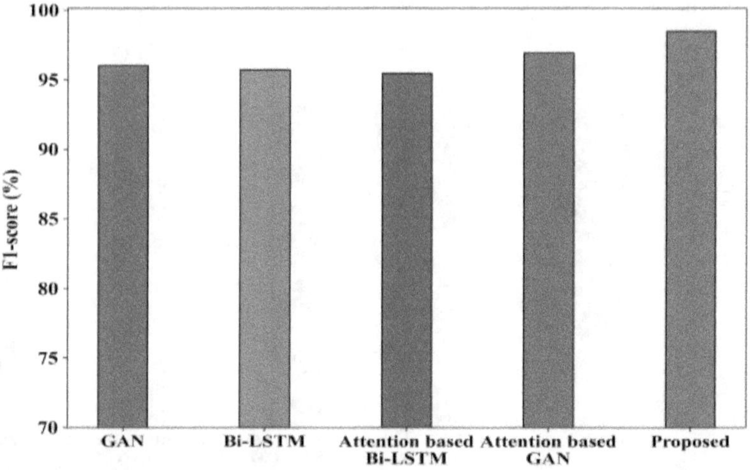

(4)

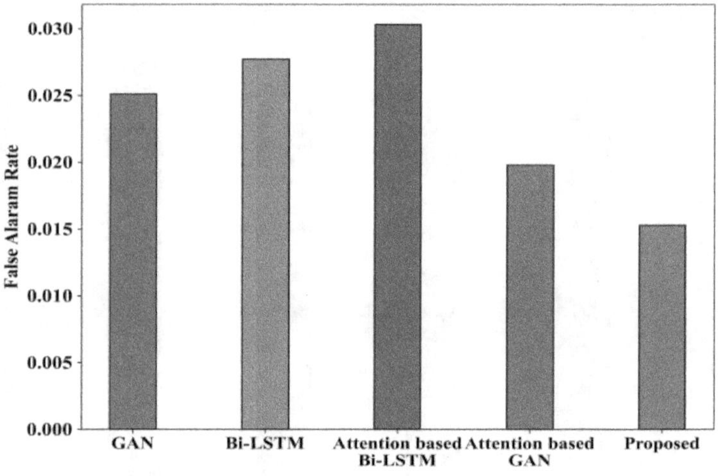

(5)

Fig. 4.6 Evaluation of the proposed At-GAN-Bi-LSTM and Traditional DL Methods' Performances

Figure 4.6 (1) compares the classification accuracy of traditional deep learning models with the proposed At-GAN-Bi-LSTM for intrusion detection in the secure IoT architecture. The baseline GAN, Bi-LSTM, and attention-based Bi-LSTM achieve accuracies of approximately 97.0%, 96.8%, and 96.7%, respectively, while the attention-based GAN improves performance to about 98.1%. The proposed At-GAN-Bi-LSTM attains the highest accuracy of nearly 99.0%, showing that the joint integration of adversarial learning, bidirectional temporal modeling, and attention mechanisms significantly improves detection reliability for IoT-based healthcare and smart grid data transmission.

Figure 4.6 (2) shows the precision comparison of traditional deep learning models and the proposed At-GAN-Bi-LSTM within the secure IoT architecture. The GAN, Bi-LSTM, and attention-based Bi-LSTM models achieve precision values of approximately 96.0%, 95.6%, and 95.4%, respectively, while the attention-based GAN improves precision to about 97.4%. The proposed At-GAN-Bi-LSTM attains the highest precision of nearly 98.6%, indicating superior capability in correctly identifying malicious traffic while minimizing false positives in IoT-based healthcare and smart grid data transmission.

Figure 4.6 (3) presents the recall comparison of traditional deep learning models and the proposed At-GAN-Bi-LSTM for intrusion detection in the secure IoT framework. The GAN, Bi-LSTM, and attention-based Bi-LSTM models achieve recall values of approximately 96.0%, 95.8%, and 95.5%, respectively, while the attention-based GAN improves recall to around 96.8%. The proposed At-GAN-Bi-LSTM achieves the highest recall of nearly 98.5%, demonstrating its superior ability to correctly identify malicious traffic and reduce missed attacks in IoT-based healthcare and smart grid environments.

Figure 4.6 (4) shows the F1-score comparison among traditional deep learning models and the proposed At-GAN-Bi-LSTM within the secure IoT intrusion detection framework. The baseline GAN, Bi-LSTM, and attention-based Bi-LSTM models achieve F1 scores of approximately 96.0%, 95.7%, and 95.5%, respectively, while the attention-based GAN improves performance to about 96.9%. The proposed At-GAN-Bi-LSTM attains the highest F1-score of nearly 98.6%.

Figure 4.6 (5) shows the FAR comparison of traditional deep learning models and the proposed At-GAN-Bi-LSTM for intrusion detection in the secure IoT framework. The baseline GAN, Bi-LSTM, and attention-based Bi-LSTM models record FAR values of approximately 0.025, 0.028, and 0.030, respectively, while the attention-based GAN reduces the FAR to about 0.020. The proposed At-GAN-Bi-LSTM achieves the lowest FAR of nearly 0.015.

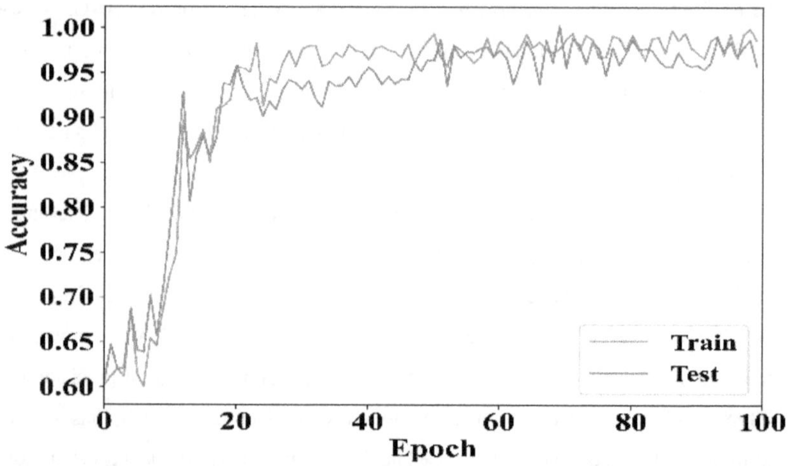

(1)

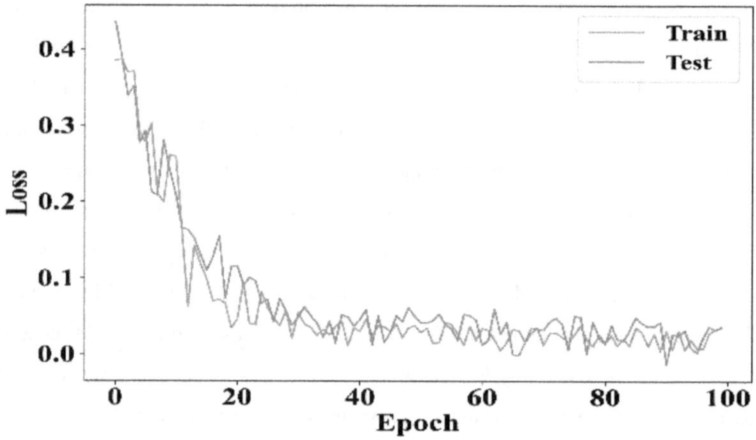

(2)

Fig. 4.7 Training and Testing Analysis of (1) Accuracy and (2) Loss Curves

Fig. 4.7 shows the training and testing performance of the proposed At-GAN-Bi-LSTM model in terms of accuracy and loss across 100 epochs. The accuracy curve shows a rapid improvement from about 60–65% in the initial epochs to nearly 98–99% for training and 96–98% for testing after around 20–30 epochs, indicating fast convergence and strong generalization. The loss decreases sharply from approximately 0.40-0.45 to below 0.05, stabilizing near 0.02-0.03 for both training and testing, which confirms effective learning with minimal overfitting and stable model optimization.

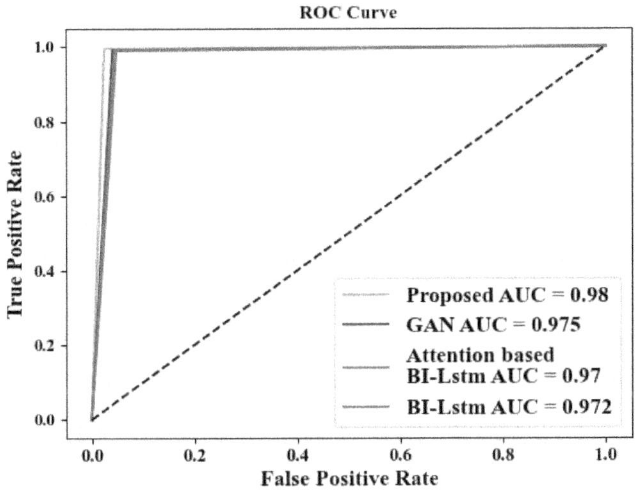

(1)

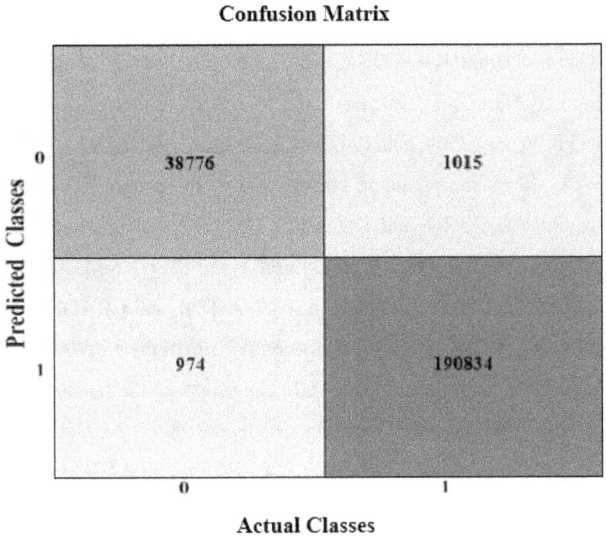

(2)

Fig. 4.8 Performance (1) ROC Curve and (2) Confusion Matrix of the Suggested At-GAN-Bi-LSTM

The ROC evaluation of the various approaches is shown in Figure 4.8 (1). The suggested At-GAN-Bi-LSTM is 0.98, the attention-based Bi-LSTM is 0.97, the GAN's AUC values are 0.975, and the Bi-LSTM is 0.972. Figure 4.8 (2) shows that 190,834 instances are expected to be normal and 38,776 instances are expected to be assaults.

4.2.4 Comparative Analysis

The suggested DL-based secure framework is compared to other approaches, such as DSAE_BILSTM, GTxChain, and GRADE, in the following subsection. Two datasets are used in the investigation, and Figure 4.9 shows the results. Many evaluation criteria are displayed. Figure 4.9 (1) presents the comparative accuracy analysis of the proposed model against existing methods across Dataset-1 and Dataset-2. The proposed approach achieves the highest accuracy of approximately 99.0% on Dataset-1 and 99.1% on Dataset-2, outperforming DSAE-BiLSTM (96.00%), GtxChain (94.00-95.00%), and GRADE (94.5-95.00%). Figure 4.9 (2) shows the FAR comparison of the proposed model with existing approaches across Dataset-1 and Dataset-2. The proposed method achieves the lowest FAR of approximately 0.015 on Dataset-1 and 0.010 on Dataset-2, outperforming DSAE-BiLSTM (0.025 / 0.023), GtxChain (0.045 / 0.047), and GRADE (0.041 / 0.042).

Figure 4.9 (3) presents the recall comparison of the proposed approach with existing techniques across Dataset-1 and Dataset-2. The proposed model achieves the highest recall of approximately 98.5% on Dataset-1 and 99.0% on Dataset-2, outperforming DSAE-BiLSTM (95.8-96.0%), GtxChain (94.2-94.8%), and GRADE (95.5-95.7%).

Figure 4.9 (4) shows the precision comparison of the proposed model against existing techniques across Dataset-1 and Dataset-2. The proposed approach attains the highest precision of approximately 98.4% on Dataset-1 and 98.9% on Dataset-2, outperforming DSAE-BiLSTM (95.7-96.3%), GtxChain (94.4-94.8%), and GRADE (94.9-95.3%).

Figure 4.9 (5) shows the F-measure comparison of the proposed model with existing approaches across Dataset-1 and Dataset-2. The proposed method achieves the highest F-measure of approximately 98.3% on Dataset-1 and 98.9% on Dataset-2, outperforming DSAE-BiLSTM (96.0-95.8%), GtxChain (94.1-94.4%), and GRADE (95.3-94.9%). The finding shows that the proposed model provides a more balanced and reliable intrusion detection performance by effectively combining high precision and recall for secure IoT-based healthcare and smart grid data transmission.

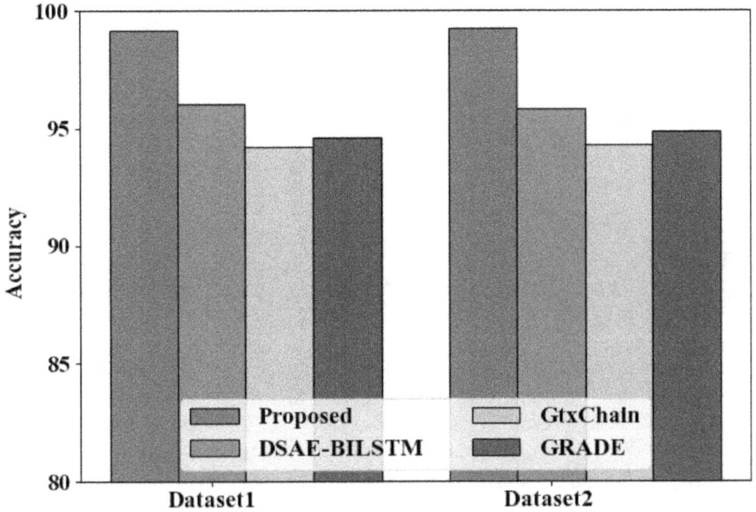
100
95
90
85
80
Accuracy
Proposed
DSAE-BILSTM
GtxChain
GRADE
Dataset1
Dataset2

(1)

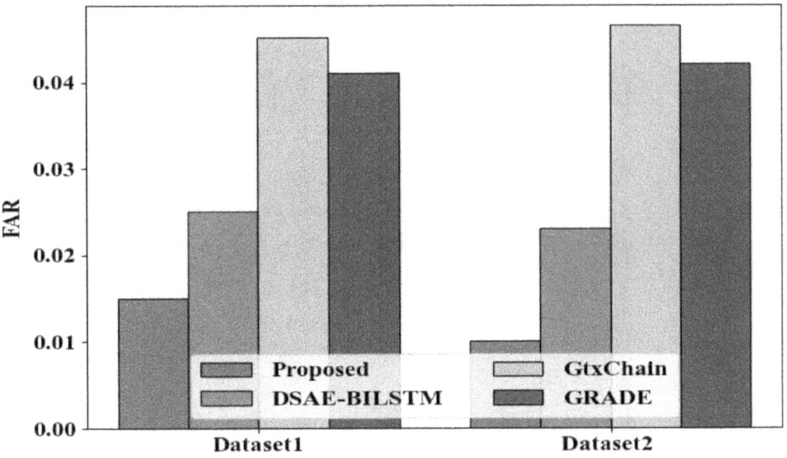
0.04
0.03
0.02
0.01
0.00
FAR
Proposed
DSAE-BILSTM
GtxChain
GRADE
Dataset1
Dataset2

(2)

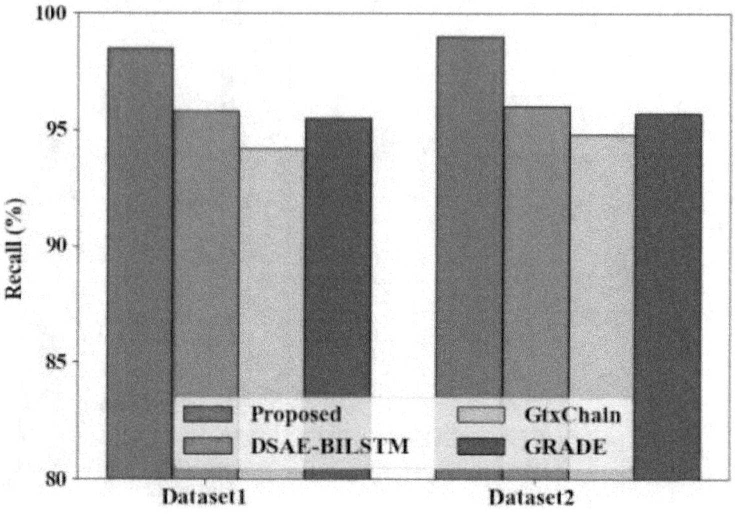

100
95
90
85
80
Recall (%)
Proposed
DSAE-BILSTM
GtxChain
GRADE
Dataset1
Dataset2

(3)

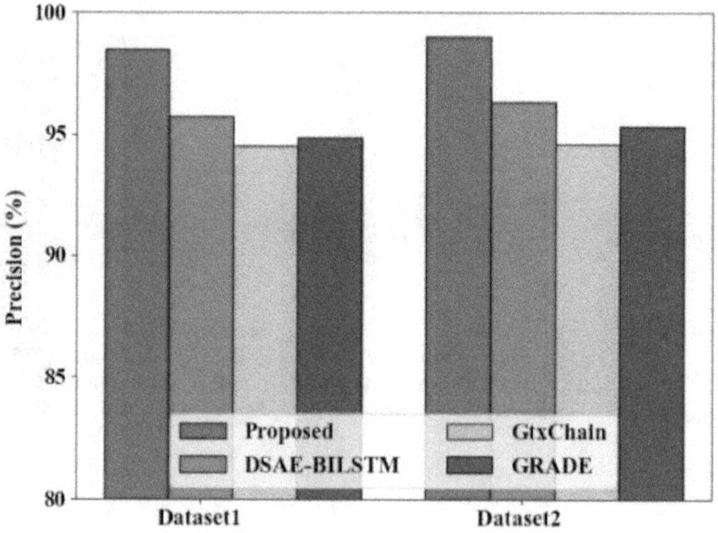

100
95
90
85
80
Precision (%)
Proposed
DSAE-BILSTM
GtxChain
GRADE
Dataset1
Dataset2

(4)

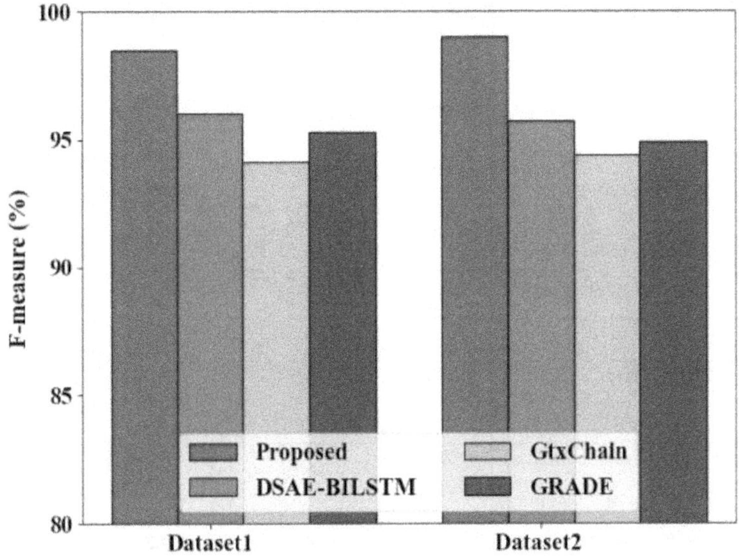

(5)

Fig. 4.9 Comparative Analysis across the Datasets

The D1 dataset's performance is displayed in Table 4.2, while the D2 dataset's performance comparison is explained in Table 4.3. In this section, RF, DT, NB, BiLSTM, and BiLSTM (Transformed) methods are compared with the suggested method (Kumar et al. 2023). The suggested method achieves good results for each data set in comparison to other methods. The suggested method yields a D1 F1-score of 99.69%, 99.85% recall, 99.9% accuracy, and 99.95% precision. The suggested method yields a 98.92% F1 score, 99.1% accuracy, 98.9% precision, and 98.91% recall for D1. It may be difficult for the conventional models to manage noisy data, recognize complex patterns, and adjust to changing assault methods. Furthermore, their dependence on manually created characteristics may restrict their capacity to glean pertinent data from unprocessed data. The safety and effectiveness of IoT-enabled healthcare providers are greatly improved by the suggested blockchain-driven DL approach. Critical patient data and platform activities are protected with high precision and low miss rates thanks to the At-GAN-BiLSTM malware detection platform's efficient identification and mitigation of possible threats. For D1, the suggested method achieves 99.9% accuracy, accuracy rates 2.09% and 0.04%

higher than those of RF and BiLSTM. For D2, the suggested method achieves 99.1% accuracy, 0.16% and 0.18% higher than that of BiLSTM and BiLSTM (Transformed).

Table 4.2 The Comparison of the D1 Dataset's Effectiveness

Methods	**Accuracy (%)**	**Precision (%)**	**Recall (%)**	**F1-measure (%)**
RF (Kumar et al. 2023)	97.81	87.55	85.43	86.41
DT (Kumar et al. 2023)	95.34	74.42	80.00	76.33
NB (Kumar et al. 2023)	77.68	76.33	77.70	72.43
BiLSTM (Kumar et al. 2023)	99.86	99.93	99.64	99.32
BiLSTM (Transformed) (Kumar et al. 2023)	99.03	99.01	96.76	97.1
Proposed	**99.9**	**99.95**	**99.85**	**99.69**

Table 4.3 The Comparison of the D2 Dataset's Effectiveness

Methods	**Accuracy (%)**	**Precision (%)**	**Recall (%)**	**F1-measure (%)**
RF (Kumar et al. 2023)	98.62	62.01	51.77	55.62
DT (Kumar et al. 2023)	98.34	77.4	62.16	64.58
NB (Kumar et al. 2023)	59.57	45.75	80.65	47
BiLSTM (Kumar et al. 2023)	98.92	86.2	81.74	82.55
BiLSTM (Transformed) (Kumar et al. 2023)	99.04	87.31	82.89	83.2
Proposed	**99.1**	**98.9**	**98.91**	**98.92**

For the D1 and D2 datasets, the suggested technique's delay is found to be 0.099 and 0.098 ms, respectively. Likewise, the suggested method attains a computational cost of 18.5% for the D1 dataset and 17% for the D2 dataset. Because the attention strategy in the GAN and Bi-LSTM systems is used, the suggested approach achieves decreased latency and processing overhead when compared to the other current methods. Likewise, for real-time tasks, the suggested method executes transactions with minimal processing cost and latency. Figure 4.10 shows the delay against computational cost analysis for the D1 and D2 datasets.

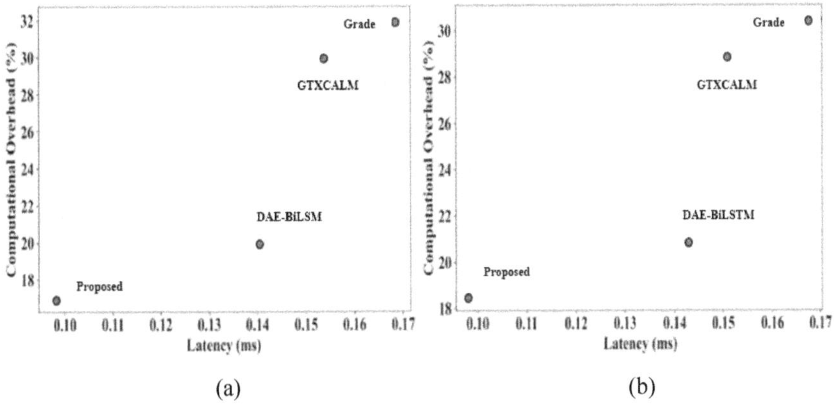

Fig. 4.10 Latency Vs. Computational Overhead for (a) D1 and (b) D2

The present investigation assessed how effectively the suggested blockchain-integrated DL approach secured IoT-based HCS while considering the D1 and D2 datasets. The evaluation on D1 showed that the At-GAN-BiLSTM system was capable of successfully identifying threats, with an accuracy rate of 99.9% in identifying an attack. This framework outperforms traditional models such as GAN, Bi-LSTM, and attention-based Bi-LSTM in terms of evaluating factors. This demonstrates how the detection effectiveness of GAN and Bi-LSTM architectures is significantly improved by incorporating attention methods. Even though security violations might have detrimental effects on medical applications, the framework's reliability in lowering FP was proved by its low FAR on D1.

When comparing the results, D1 performed marginally superior to D2, even though the strategy capacity for generalization was evident on both datasets. With the incorporation of the Ethereum Blockchain which provided confidentiality of information and protection from identity and MITM attacks, the system's cybersecurity was further strengthened. Additionally, problems with data storing and retrieving were successfully fixed by IPFS implementation. These results suggest that, in a range of scenarios covered by D1 and D2, the suggested At-GAN-BiLSTM framework is a successful intrusion identification method for IoT-based HCS that offers enhanced safety, precision, and durability.

Flexibility and adaptability are necessary for larger medical centers that incorporate additional IoT nodes and detectors, and the suggested At-GAN-BiLSTM approach is designed to effectively manage massive data volumes. The suggested method creates a distributed framework that facilitates further information transfers yet preserves the confidentiality and integrity of data by combining Blockchain technology, particularly Ethereum, with IPFS for distributed storage. The framework's attention-based approach optimizes resource allocation, enabling real-time intrusion identification and adaptability as further IoT nodes are connected. Additionally, the At-GAN-BiLSTM model improves flexibility without appreciably lowering latency by enabling batch processing and periodic updates. Table 4.4 shows an evaluation of the suggested and cutting-edge methods.

Table 4.4 Comparison of the Suggested and Existing Techniques

Authors and Ref	Methods	Accuracy Score
Kumar et al. (2021)	TP2SF framework	-
Neelakandan et al. (2022)	A blockchain with a DL model	95.2% Accuracy
Salim et al. (2021)	LSTM	91% Accuracy –BoT-IoT dataset
Ferrag et al. (2021)	DL model FL with the Blockchain model	-
Sharma et al. (2021)	Blockchain with ANN model	95% Accuracy for the BoT-IoT dataset
Singh et al. (2022)	Privacy preservation of IoT-based HCS using FL and Blockchain	Accuracy (95.76% for Bot-IoT, 90.06% accuracy for MQTT, and 98.87% for TON-IoT dataset)
Alkadi et al. (2020)	DBF with BiLSTM	97.26% and 96.71% accuracy for UNSW-NB15 and BoT-IoT
Unal et al. (2021)	FL model with the Blockchain	-

Kumar et al. (2023)	A ZKP method using the DL	99.03% and 99.04% accuracy for CICIDS-2017 and ToN-IoT
Cai et al. (2023)	GTxChain	-
Jadav N. K. et al. (2023)	GRADE	98.44% accuracy
Proposed	**At-GAN-Bi-LSTM DL model**	**Accuracy of D1 = 99.9%** **Accuracy of D2 = 99.1%**

Table 4.4 shows the comparative analysis of proposed models with existing models. In this section existing models were selected because they represent state-of-the-art security models that are closest in scope to this study in terms of (i) protecting IoT data, (ii) integrating blockchain or privacy-preserving mechanisms, and/or (iii) employing DL/FL for intrusion detection. Specifically, Kumar et al. (2021), Neelakandan et al. (2022), Salim et al. (2021), and Ferrag et al. (2021) were included because they explicitly address secure IoT/healthcare data transmission using blockchain-enabled trust, cryptographic protection, or DL/FL-based detection on widely used benchmark datasets such as ToN-IoT and BoT-IoT. In addition, works such as Alkadi et al. (2020), Sharma et al. (2021), Singh et al. (2022), Unal et al. (2021), Cai et al. (2024), and Jadav et al. (2023) were considered because they combine blockchain-driven protection and learning-based detection (or related scalable architectures), providing relevant reference points for benchmarking detection accuracy and deployment feasibility in IoT settings.

The proposed model achieves superior performance because it jointly addresses security assurance and learning-based attack detection in a single pipeline. On D1, the proposed At-GAN-BiLSTM achieves 99.9% accuracy, 99.95% precision, 99.85% recall, and a 99.69% F1-score, while on D2 it achieves 99.1% accuracy with 98.9% precision and a 98.92% F1-score, demonstrating consistent generalization across heterogeneous IoT traffic distributions. This improvement is driven by two key design choices: (i) privacy-preserving and tamper-resistant communication, achieved through the Ethereum blockchain with ZKP-based authentication and IPFS-backed distributed storage to prevent identity/MITM risks and single-point failures, and (ii) attention-guided generative-sequential modeling, where At-GAN strengthens representation learning of normal/attack distributions and BiLSTM captures bidirectional temporal dependencies in network flows.

Beyond detection quality, the model remains suitable for real-time IoT deployment because the measured delay is 0.099 ms (D1) and 0.098 ms (D2) with a computational overhead of 18.5% (D1) and 17% (D2), indicating that the added security controls do not compromise responsiveness.

By combining ZKP-based device authentication, IPFS-enabled distributed storage, and EBC-assisted DL, this study presents a novel method for securely transmitting IoT data. In theory, by guaranteeing the confidentiality of information and connection reliability, distributed systems like Blockchain and IPFS can improve IoT cybersecurity. A new frontier in merging generative adversarial networks with bidirectional LSTMs for detecting abnormalities in IoT networks is the combination with an At-GAN-Bi-LSTM approach to real-time threats of risks. In practice, the suggested approach provides a strong, scalable foundation for sectors like smart city development and medical treatment, offering a very efficient way to secure IoT sensors and infrastructure.

4.2.5 Security Analysis

This section evaluates the security strength of the proposed framework under various adversarial threats: impersonation, insider compromise, MITM, replay, spoofing, Sybil, data tampering, smart contract exploitation, DDoS, key compromise, and traffic analysis.

(a) Impersonation Attack: The hacker A carries out activities as authorized S_i by sharing ID_{Si} and M_{Si} to V_e getting the P_k. Then, the Ts_i obtains the request from ID_{Si} and V_e analyzes the M_{Si} and Ts_i. When the Ts_i is matched successfully, then the ZKP is carried out. When the matching Ts_i is not successful, the process ends. Therefore, the suggested EBC's resistance to the impersonating attack was effectively demonstrated.

(b) Insider Attack: The hacker A might be allowed, and it is aware of data like as ID_{Si} and M_{Si}. However, the ID_{Si} cannot be calculated because of Ts_i across ZKP. Thus, it has been demonstrated that the suggested EBC is resistant to insider threats.

(c) MITM and Replay Attacks: The hacker A acquires data through unreliable sources. ID_{Si} and M_{Si} executes the MITM and replay attacks. Then, from the insecure channel S_i

must calculate the Ts_i. To achieve accuracy, the procedure requires greater processing resources Ts_i over ZKP. ZKP is a complicated procedure that requires precise response prediction. Thus, it has been demonstrated that the suggested EBC is resistant to reversal and MITM attacks.

(d) Spoofing Attack: Possible inducing of spoofing: --replacing device identification code, MAC address, or network password. In the presented model, blockchain registration and ZKP complete each other for spoofing resistance. Even with a MAC address spoof attack, authentication is impossible without valid ZKP proof of the true device. As a result, the spoofing attacks are declined at the time of authentication.

(e) Sybil Attack: A Sybil attack is a severe threat for IoT networks when an attacker makes up many bogus identities to tamper with trust mechanisms and consume network resources. Device registration is approved through the blockchain network in our model, with its identity bound to irrevocable records saved within Ethereum. As blockchain technology prevents duplicate and unauthorized registration of identity, Sybil identities are hardly provided into the system. Thus, Sybil attacks are defended by decentralizing identity checks.

(f) Data Tampering Attack: Thus, data tampering attacks intend to alter health care information while it is being transmitted or stored. The presented framework is not easily tampered with due to blockchain and IPFS, where the content addressing is used. IPFS and blockchain: each time data gets stored on IPFS, it is assigned a unique hash, and that hash itself is sent to the blockchain. Any change to the file in storage changes the hash, and tampering would be immediately detectable. Thus, it guaranteed the data storage level and ledger-level integrity.

(g) Smart Contract Exploitation: Weaknesses include re-entrancy, overflow/underflow, and access control weaknesses in smart contracts. Smart contracts are used to enable access control policies and role-based permission to be implemented for registering a device, authenticating the device, and accessing data within the system. Additionally, transparency on the blockchain allows for auditing of contract interactions. As such, notwithstanding potential smart contract attacks, the framework mitigates exploitation risks by regulating access and tracking transactions.

(h) DDoS Attack: Since resource constraint is a feature of IoT networks, they are vulnerable to DDoS attacks. Nevertheless, the integrity provided by blockchains may result in overheads under high load. To tackle this, the proposed framework integrates a DL-based IDS (At-GAN-BiLSTM) that alerts for abnormal traffic patterns such as volumetric flooding and unusual request rates. Malicious nodes can also be blocked or isolated once detected. Therefore, the framework exhibits strengthened resistance to DDoS using intelligent detection and reduction.

(i) Key Compromise Attack: In the event of key compromise, an attacker could have access to private keys or session authentication via malware or device theft. The proposed system mitigates the effect of insider attacks and raises resistance by decreasing the exposure of sensitive credentials via ZKP authentication. Because ZKP is not explicitly transmitting secret keys, thereby diminishing the risk of key leakage through channels. In addition, blockchain-enabled ID records provide a way to revoke and blacklist compromised devices. Therefore, the framework secures by minimizing credentials and revocation support.

(j) Analysis of Traffic and Privacy Leaks: Traffic analysis attacks aim to deduce patient sensitive information from communication patterns, timing, and metadata. In our scheme, blockchain restricts unauthorized data access, and IPFS out-of-chain preserves the encrypted healthcare information. In addition, ZKP authentication prevents device secrets and identity ownership from being leaked in verification. Thus, less metadata is disclosed to prevent possible privacy leakage, and cryptographic authentication is enforced.

Table 4.5 Summary of the Attack Resistance Properties

Attack Vector	Threat Objective	Mitigation Mechanism in Proposed Framework
Impersonation	Fake device login	ZKP authentication and verifier validation
Insider attack	Abuse legitimate access	ZKP secrecy and blockchain traceability
MITM	Modify/redirect messages	ZKP, session integrity and timestamp
Replay	Reuse old messages	Timestamp and session binding
Spoofing	Fake MAC/identity	Blockchain registration and ZKP
Sybil	Multiple fake identities	Immutable blockchain identity validation
Data tampering	Modify medical records	Ethereum immutability and IPFS hash checking
Smart contract attack	Exploit smart contract vulnerabilities	Access control and auditability
DDoS	Flood network resources	IDS detection and malicious node isolation
Key compromise	Stolen keys/credentials	ZKP prevents secret exposure and revocation
Traffic analysis	Infer patient data	Encryption + ZKP + minimal metadata exposure

Table 4.5 shows a summary of the attack resistance properties. In summary, the proposed blockchain-empowered DL framework can ensure multi-layer integrity for an IoT-based healthcare system through the seamless integration of ZKP authentication, non-repudiable blockchain logging, secure IPFS storage, and intelligent DL-based invasion detection. The framework outperforms conventional centralized security architectures in resistance to classical IoT assaults as well as blockchain-native threats (in contrast, offering confidentiality, integrity, and secure access control of patient-related healthcare data).

4.3 Proposed Model-2: Enhancing the LoRaWAN P/S IoT Data Sharing Model using Middleman for Smart Grid Application

4.3.1 Experimental Setup

This section describes the experimental setup adopted to evaluate the proposed LoRaWAN–MQTT–based communication model for secure healthcare and smart grid IoT data transmission. The experiments were conducted using a network-level simulation model, implemented in the NS-3 simulator, which accurately represents LoRaWAN end devices, gateways, network servers, and MQTT-based P/S communication.

The simulated network consists of LoRaWAN end devices acting as IoT sensors, one or more LoRaWAN gateways, a network server, and an MQTT broker integrated at the gateway/server level. End devices periodically generate healthcare or smart grid data packets and transmit them to the gateway using LoRaWAN. The gateway forwards the received packets to the network server, which publishes the data to the MQTT broker. Subscriber applications receive the data based on topic subscriptions.

The NS-3 was selected for this study because it provides accurate and fine-grained modeling of low-power wireless communication protocols, making it particularly suitable for evaluating LoRaWAN-based IoT networks. The simulator supports detailed physical and MAC layer configurations, including duty-cycle constraints, spreading factors, transmission power, and Adaptive Data Rate (ADR) mechanisms, which are critical for realistic IoT performance analysis. In addition, NS-3 enables scalable and reproducible experimentation across diverse deployment scenarios such as urban, rural, and hybrid environments, allowing controlled variation of network parameters and node density. Its modular architecture facilitates seamless integration with higher-layer protocols, such as MQTT-based P/S communication, enabling end-to-end evaluation of both network performance and application-level behavior.

The resultant nodes are going to be dispersed at random toward the terminal, which will consist of a disc surrounding it, to allow for the writers to prepare for employing LoRaWAN links. For each study, the writers state that the end nodes and the interface are no more than 2000 meters. To allow communication between the gateway and the broker, the writers utilize a point-to-point connection. It is assumed that the end nodes, agent, and gateway are all static. Although the first geographic parameters of the LoRaWAN unit had been set up to comply with EU standards, the writers had to increase the standard frequency range for the majority of the experiments from 1% to 50%.

This action was taken since the gateway is unable to communicate with the destination endpoints having a duty cycle of 1%. When the channel is successfully broadcast, a Class-C LoRa device can continue to respond to it.

The experiments were implemented using NS-3 version 3.38 with the LoRaWAN module enabled. NS-3 was executed on a Linux environment, and MQTT functionality was integrated using a lightweight broker model.

Table 4.6 shows the parameters were selected to reflect realistic LoRaWAN deployments in healthcare and smart grid scenarios while allowing scalability analysis under increasing node density and traffic load (Muneer et al. 2024, Singh et al. 2015, Kumar et al. 2023).

Table 4.6 Simulation Parameters and Settings

Parameter	Value
Simulator	NS-3 (v3.38)
Network Type	LoRaWAN + MQTT
Frequency Band	868 MHz
Bandwidth	125 kHz
Spreading Factor	SF7–SF12
Transmission Power	14 dBm
Duty Cycle	1% (baseline), extended for evaluation
Number of End Devices	10, 50, 200
Number of Gateways	1–3
Deployment Scenarios	Urban, Rural, Hybrid
Packet Size	50 bytes
Traffic Model	Periodic sensing traffic
MQTT QoS Level	QoS-1
Simulation Time	1000 seconds

4.3.2 Experimental Outcome

The following section displays the results generated by our 30-times-repeated NS-3 modelling. The lines of error, demonstrating the data's statistical significance, are visible to the writers. The result is 95% likely and in the range of average ±1.96 standard error. Average delay, publish delay, PDR, and latency are widely adopted performance measurements used to evaluate the performance of IoT communication systems based on LoRaWAN (Victor Seoane et al. 2021).

(a) Node Average Count Effect: The total amount of nodes that would constitute our broker's users (P/S) was changed for this experiment.

As the total amount of accessible nodes increases, Figure 4.11 illustrates how long it requires to broadcast the information for every subscriber. This is because more individuals have subscribed to the topics because of the additional nodes. To deliver the published information to them, the agent must transmit separate unicast transmission messages to every subscriber over the router without adhering to the duty cycle of the gateway. Consequently, these results consider the bandwidth constraints of LoRaWAN for particular uses. For example, assuming real-time data interchange and activities are needed, subsequently boosting the number of LoRa terminals would significantly impact the results. Specifically, a congestion of about 20 endpoints is caused by the delay (for example, transmitting a payload takes more than 5 seconds).

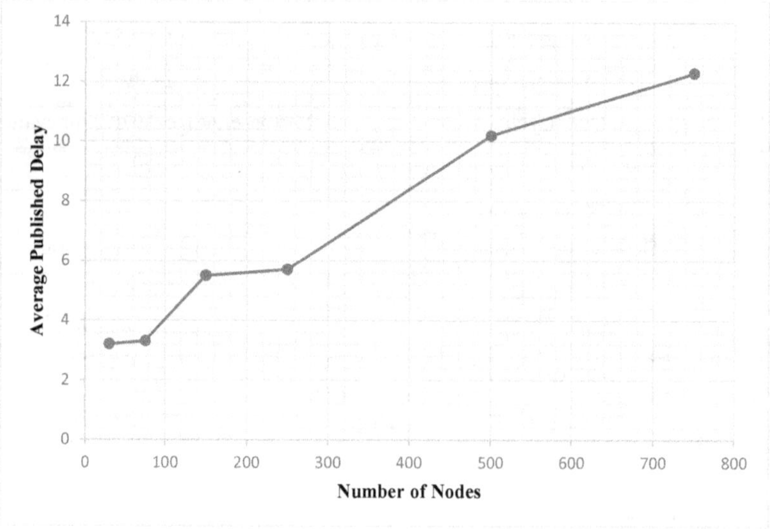

Fig. 4.11 Average Delay of Several Nodes

In the US, where data transfer happens every 15 minutes, electronic meters might be considered one of the uses for the distributed power system (Cai et al. 2023). Data (that is physical values) need to be collected and transmitted at an interval of each hour or two by multiple distributed sensors. This is not an issue, however network is less efficient if data have to be retrieved at small intervals such as: once a minute or second. It is preferable to organize the data providers in these situations by incorporating numerous interfaces.

(b) Rural vs. Urban Environment Node Count Effect: Apart from the modeled environment's inclusion of structures, the methods employed in the present investigation are comparable to those employed in studies on the effects of sensor amount. The addition of grid-arranged structures may be an attempt by the creators to replicate an urban environment. The terminal endpoints are arranged in a circle having the center of the array in the middle. The typical roadway width is 25 meters, and each building is 130 m × 60 m with four floors. a circle having a topic number of 50 and an outer diameter of 1000 meters. Figure 4.12 illustrates the extended mean publishing delay for gadgets in the rural scenario. Since additional packets can be obtained, the processing time for each packet increases with the package performance margin. The packets are anyway lost in cities, due to obstructed line of sight.

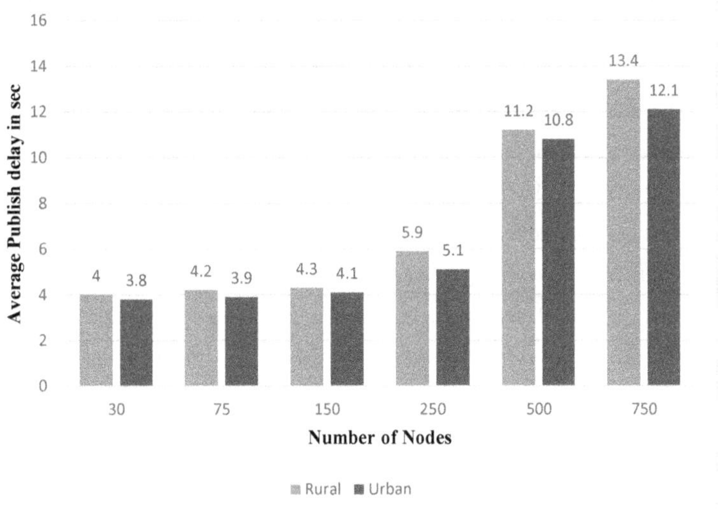

Fig. 4.12 Comparative Analysis of Average Publish Delay of Rural and Urban over the Nodes

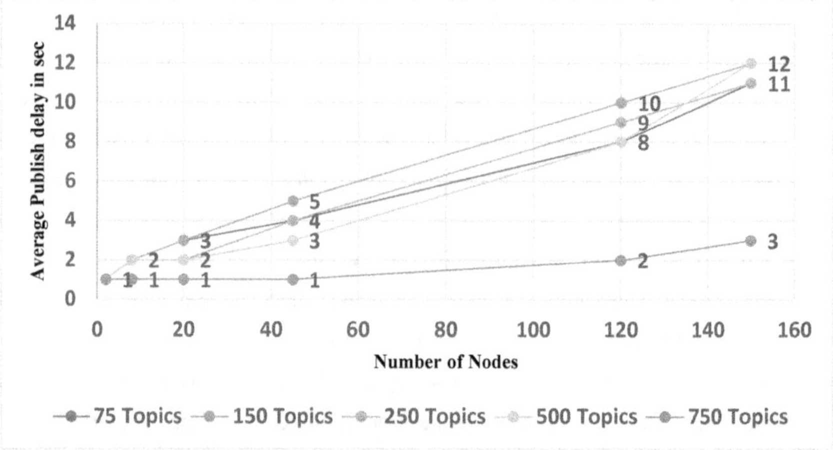

Fig. 4.13 Impact of Increasing Node Count on Average Publish in an MQTT-based P/S System

(c) The Impact of Subject Density on Publication Postponement: Investigators adjusted the total number of subjects provided in the present investigation according to the number of terminal nodes. To evaluate the network's efficacy, the researchers changed the number of subjects from 10 to 200. Every end gadget is dispersed at random inside a 1000-meter-radius circle. The entrance is in the middle of the circle. Figure 4.13 shows that the average publication delay increases for each number of final equipment when 10 subjects are used compared to 200. The count of subscribers explains this. This suggests that whenever there remains the identical total of nodes but fewer subjects, then there will be subjects that have greater subscribers collectively. This increases the average delay since more unicast packets are required for reaching every subscribing node separately. Nonetheless, these experiments showed that the article number only matters when a particular subject contains a substantial number of subscribed nodes. Otherwise, it might not have an impact on the performance's scalability.

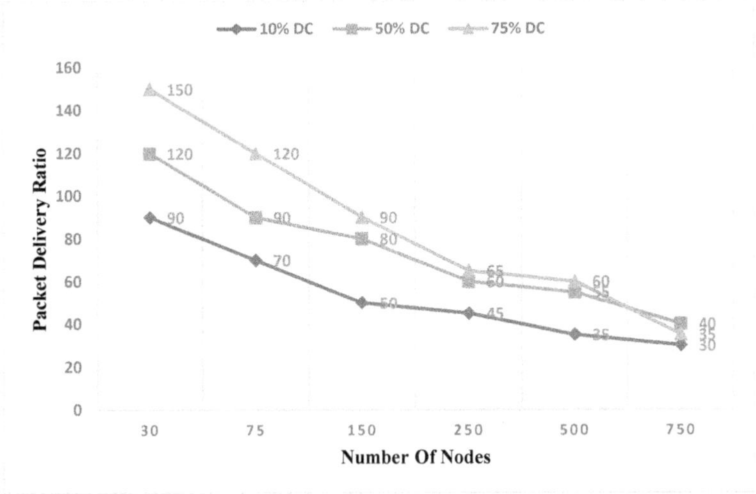

Fig. 4.14 Effect of Increasing Node Density on PDR in an IoT Communication Network

(d) Duty Cycle Effects on PDR: The duty cycle (DC) of the router was changed by the authors to conduct the present study while keeping other factors unchanged. Our trials employed different amounts of nodes and ten topics. The DC scores of 1%, 10%, 25%, and 50% were used by the researchers. All nodes are dispersed at random inside a 1000-meter-radius circle. In the middle of the round area stands the gateway.

Figure 4.14 shows that when the gateway's accessible DC rises, so does the packet transmission ratio. This is because there is a correlation between the DC and the transmission time. A greater wait before the device may start receiving again is indicated by a smaller DC percentage. The findings demonstrate that DC has a significant impact on efficiency and that, beyond 10 nodes, the PDR begins to decrease. Given the current LoRa standards, a significant constraint in Europe or the US is a minimum voltage of 50% DC to completely achieve the PDR.

(e) Range Influences on Publishing Delays: In one such study, ending devices were dispersed at random and the circle's radius was changed. The investigators selected an area of 2000 m, 4000 m, 6000 m, 8000 m, and 12000 m, considering these are standard ranges for LoRaWAN transmissions. The investigators used 50 participants altogether with a 75% DC. It was made sure that every communication was sent in order to keep an eye on how the system was operating.

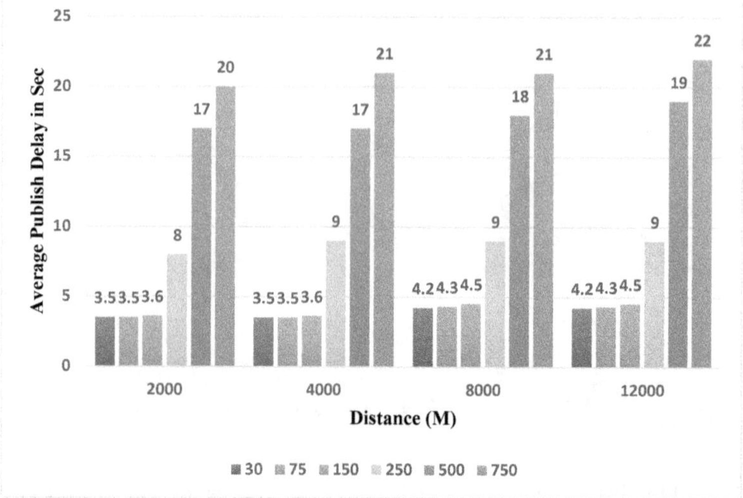

Fig. 4.15 Impact of Increasing Distance on Average Publish Delay in an MQTT-Based P/S System

Whenever the range of delays is expanded, Figure 4.15 shows that the average publishing delay significantly improves. The delay has increased since unique SF levels are utilized for every single unicast message. LoRaWAN chooses the proper SF based on the final node's distance from the gateway. Gadgets that are closer to the gateway receive an SF of 7, while those that are farther away have an SF of 12. Greater publication delays result from the usage of larger SF, which causes longer Time-On-Air (TOA) numbers. Prior experiments have demonstrated that the average publish latency increases in tandem with the number of nodes.

(f) Urban vs. Rural Environments and the Impact of Range: The study of the urban variant of the distance influences on average published delay study is being conducted as part of this inquiry. To simulate a city's atmosphere, the endpoint was organized in a grid by the writers. The grid's lines represent the pathways, and the structures are placed among them. The writers use 50 themes and 75% DC.

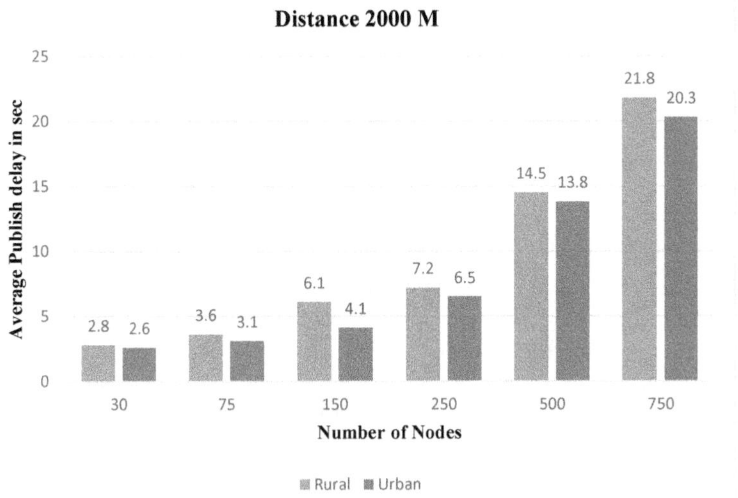

Distance 2000 M
Average Publish delay in sec
25
20
15
10
5
0
2.8
2.6
3.6
3.1
6.1
4.1
7.2
6.5
14.5
13.8
21.8
20.3
30
75
150
250
500
750
Number of Nodes
Rural
Urban

(1)

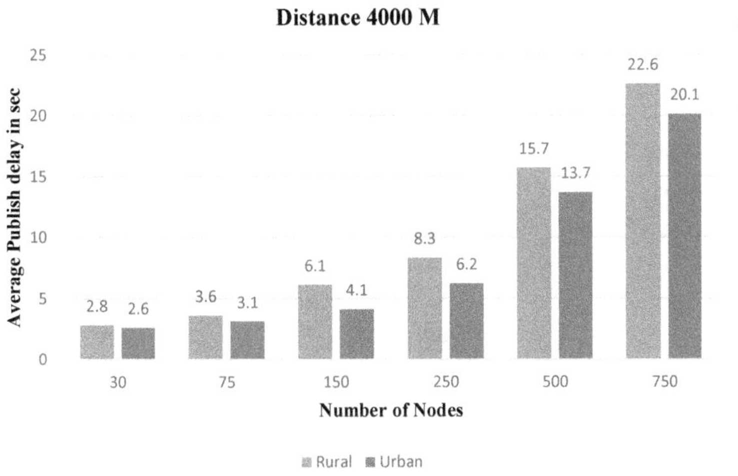

Distance 4000 M
Average Publish delay in sec
25
20
15
10
5
0
2.8
2.6
3.6
3.1
6.1
4.1
8.3
6.2
15.7
13.7
22.6
20.1
30
75
150
250
500
750
Number of Nodes
Rural
Urban

(2)

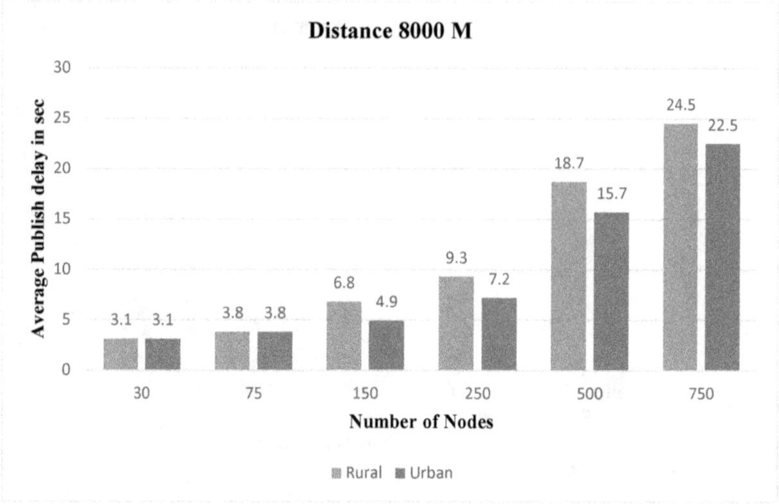

(3)

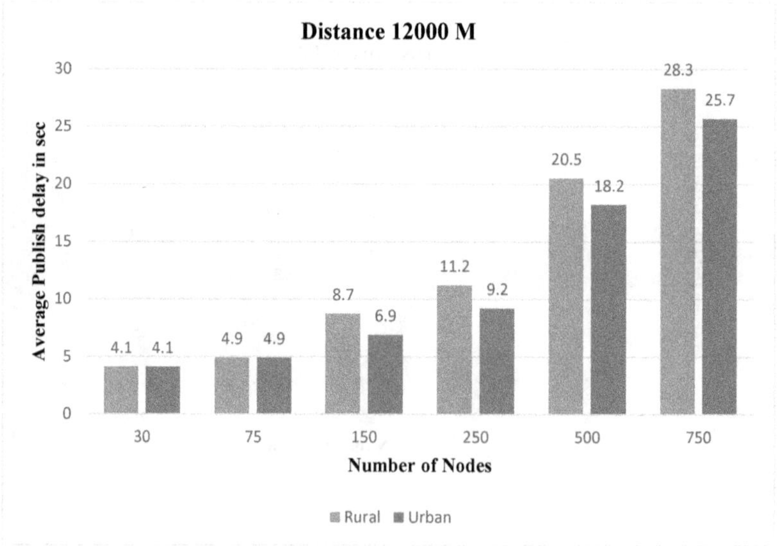

(4)

Fig. 4.16 Comparative Analysis of Rural and Urban Areas of Average Published Delay over the Distance

Figure 4.16 displays the average publication latency at different distances as the node size increases. The authors observe that a situation containing buildings has an average publishing delay that is longer than the scenario without structures. This is the result of a lower level of packet delivery. In other words, it maintains the total publication delays, that will reduce when additional messages are lost, since the normal publication delays reflect the typical time needed to post to each subscriber. The loss occurs since LoRaWAN is particularly susceptible to barriers. LoRaWAN can only function at its maximum range if there is a continuous association between the entering and the receiving end. The total average publication delay for both scenarios decreases with greater distance, as seen in Figure 4.16. This occurs because of additional obstacles obstructing the direct line of vision between the terminal device and the point of entry.

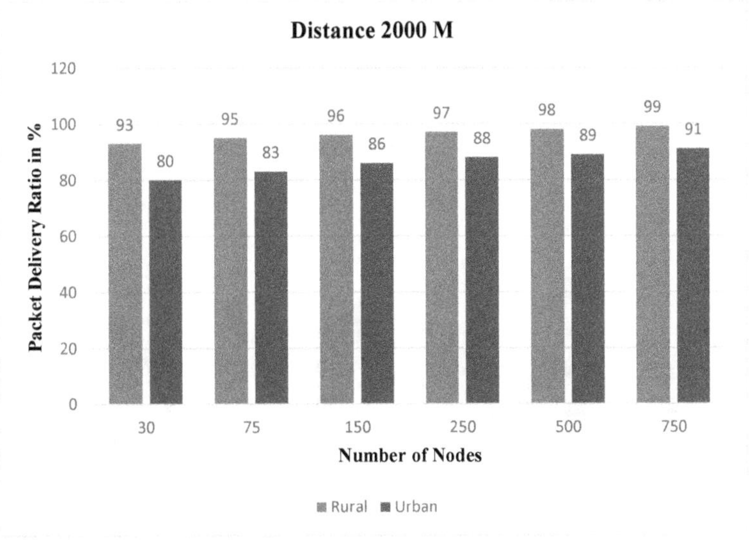

(1)

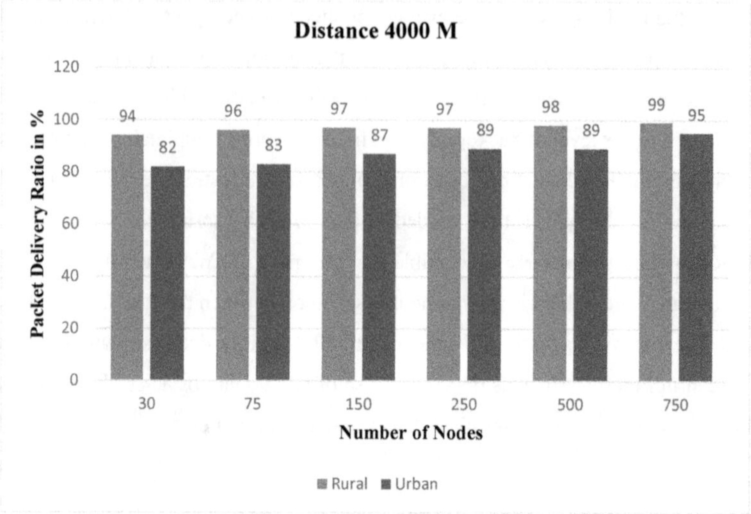
Distance 4000 M
120
100
80
60
40
20
0
94
82
96
83
97
87
97
89
98
89
99
95
30
75
150
250
500
750
Packet Delivery Ratio in %
Number of Nodes
Rural
Urban

(2)

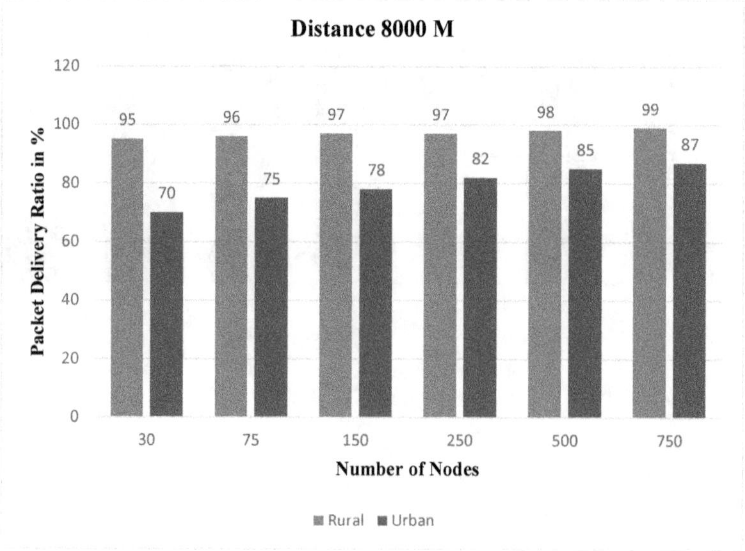
Distance 8000 M
120
100
80
60
40
20
0
95
70
96
75
97
78
97
82
98
85
99
87
30
75
150
250
500
750
Packet Delivery Ratio in %
Number of Nodes
Rural
Urban

(3)

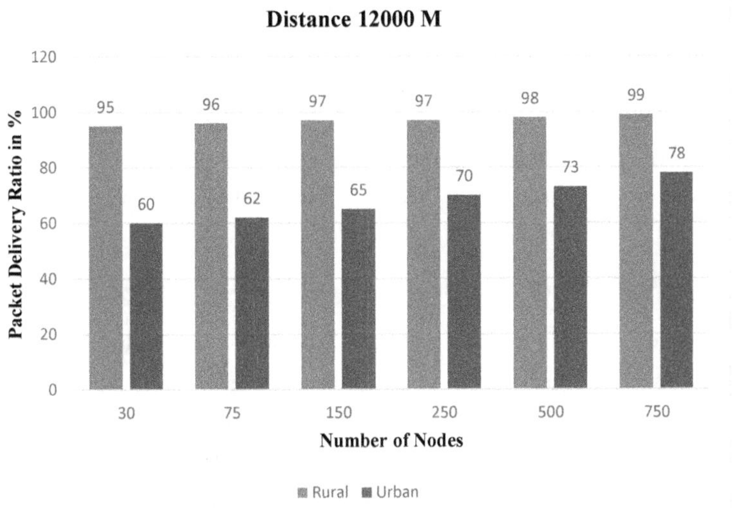

(4)

Fig. 4.17 Comparative Analysis of Rural and Urban Areas of PDR over the Distance

The packet delivery rate remains above 90% in a remote region with no systems, as illustrated in Figure 4.17. This holds true regardless of how many terminal devices there are or how far apart they are. This is because, while in a straight line of perception, LoRaWAN may operate over 15 kilometers distant. This is not possible whenever writers incorporate structures in the situation at hand. The remote PDR condition is nearly 98%, as shown in Figure 4.17, but it continues to decline as the distance increases. The reason for this is that a longer distance also makes it more likely to exist; there will be several structures across the gateway with the terminal device.

CHAPTER 5

Conclusion and Future Scope

This chapter is the summary of the original contributions made and the major conclusions drawn from the proposed work. This chapter also identifies avenues for future research.

5.1 Conclusion

The rapid proliferation of IoT technologies in critical domains such as healthcare and smart grids has intensified concerns related to data security, privacy preservation, and communication efficiency. IoT-based HCS handles highly sensitive patient information, while smart grid infrastructures demand reliable and low-latency data transmission for operational stability. Traditional centralized security mechanisms and communication architectures have proven inadequate in addressing the combined challenges of scalability, real-time intrusion detection, and secure data exchange. In response to these challenges, this research was guided by four core objectives: (i) analyzing security challenges in existing IoT architectures, (ii) applying secure data access and exchange methodologies, (iii) proposing a novel secure IoT architecture, and (iv) evaluating the performance of the proposed architecture against existing solutions.

To address the first and second objectives, this dissertation systematically examined prevailing security vulnerabilities in IoT environments, including unauthorized access, data tampering, privacy leakage, and high FAR in IDS. Existing centralized and signature-based solutions were found to be limited in adaptability and resilience. Building on this analysis, the study proposed two complementary security-driven models tailored to different IoT application contexts.

The first proposed model focuses on secure data transmission and intrusion detection in IoT-HCS. This architecture integrates an Ethereum-based Blockchain framework with ZKP authentication, IPFS for decentralized storage, and a hybrid At-GAN-BiLSTM DL model for intrusion detection. Blockchain ensures tamper-proof data handling and decentralized trust, and ZKP preserves device and data privacy, while IPFS mitigates single-point-of-failure risks. The At-GAN-BiLSTM model enhances anomaly detection by addressing data imbalance through adversarial learning, capturing temporal dependencies via bidirectional LSTM, and emphasizing critical traffic patterns using an attention mechanism. Experimental evaluation on CICIDS-2018 (D1) and ToN-IoT (D2) datasets demonstrated superior performance, achieving 99.9% accuracy on D1 and 99.1% accuracy on D2, with high precision, recall, and F1-scores, alongside low FAR. These results confirm that the integration of Blockchain with advanced DL significantly strengthens security and privacy in IoT-based healthcare environments, thereby fulfilling the third and fourth research objectives.

The second proposed model addresses secure and efficient communication for IoT-based intelligent grid systems through an enhanced LoRaWAN–MQTT P/S architecture. While LoRaWAN offers long-range and low-power communication, it suffers from scalability, congestion, and resource management challenges under dense deployments. To overcome these limitations, the proposed framework incorporates ADR optimization, congestion-aware scheduling, and MQTT-based topic management to improve network efficiency and reliability. Extensive simulations conducted using the NS-3 network simulator demonstrated that the proposed LoRaWAN–MQTT model significantly improves communication performance. The results show a reduction in mean publish delay by approximately 35% and an increase in PDR from about 85% to 96% compared to conventional LoRaWAN implementations. These findings validate that the proposed communication architecture effectively supports secure, low-latency, and scalable data transmission in smart grid IoT scenarios.

Based on the obtained results, this study provides the following practical recommendations. First, security-critical IoT deployments such as HCS should adopt blockchain-assisted authentication and decentralized storage to ensure data integrity and patient privacy. Second, intrusion detection mechanisms should leverage hybrid DL architectures that combine generative modeling, temporal learning, and attention mechanisms to improve detection accuracy while reducing false alarms. Third, large-scale IoT communication infrastructures should integrate LoRaWAN with MQTT-based P/S models to enhance scalability, reduce latency, and improve delivery reliability under high node density. These recommendations can guide system designers, healthcare providers, and smart grid operators in deploying secure and efficient IoT solutions.

Beyond practical implications, this research also makes significant contributions to theory and the body of knowledge. First, it advances the theoretical understanding of Blockchain–DL co-design by demonstrating how decentralized trust mechanisms and attention-driven sequential learning can be jointly optimized for IoT security. Second, the study contributes a unified architectural perspective that bridges security, privacy, and communication efficiency across heterogeneous IoT applications, which have been largely treated in isolation in prior literature. Third, the integration of adversarial learning with bidirectional temporal modeling and attention mechanisms provides a novel theoretical framework for handling imbalanced and evolving IoT traffic patterns. Finally, the work extends existing IoT communication theory by empirically validating how P/S paradigms enhance LoRaWAN scalability and reliability, thereby enriching the theoretical foundation for LPWAN-based IoT systems.

5.2 Future Scope

The proposed architectures demonstrate strong security and performance improvements; several future research directions emerge directly from the obtained results and system limitations. First, the computational overhead associated with Blockchain operations and DL inference can be further optimized by exploring lightweight cryptographic schemes, model compression techniques, and edge-accelerated inference, thereby improving real-time responsiveness in resource-constrained environments. Second, the strong detection accuracy achieved by the At-GAN-BiLSTM model motivates the exploration of federated and collaborative learning frameworks, where models can be trained across distributed IoT nodes without sharing raw data, further enhancing privacy and scalability.

Third, the promising communication performance of the LoRaWAN–MQTT framework suggests extending the proposed architecture to large-scale multi-gateway deployments and cross-regional smart grid infrastructures, with dynamic gateway placement and mobility-aware scheduling. Fourth, future work may integrate adaptive, self-healing security mechanisms that leverage RL to dynamically respond to emerging attack patterns observed in real-time traffic. Finally, the proposed architectures can be generalized and validated across additional application domains such as industrial automation, smart cities, precision agriculture, and financial IoT systems, enabling broader applicability and comparative evaluation across heterogeneous IoT ecosystems.

www.ingramcontent.com/pod-product-compliance
Lightning Source LLC
LaVergne TN
LVHW010731061126
851857LV00014B/1433